INSPIRED COURAGE

BREAKING
through *your*
BARRIERS to
SUCCESS

CONNIE PHELAN

FriesenPress

One Printers Way
Altona, MB R0G 0B0
Canada

www.friesenpress.com

ISBN
978-1-03-910589-8 (Hardcover)
978-1-03-910588-1 (Paperback)
978-1-03-910590-4 (eBook)

1. BUSINESS & ECONOMICS, MOTIVATIONAL

2. SELF-HELP, PERSONAL GROWTH / SUCCESS

3. SELF-HELP, MOTIVATIONAL & INSPIRATIONAL

Distributed to the trade by The Ingram Book Company

Cover design by Lorne Grandison
Author photograph by Robert Klemm Photography

Inspired Courage is available for bulk purchase for your company, organization, educational institution, athletic team, gift, or sales promotional use. For more information, please contact connie@firepowerseminars.com.

Contents

For Karen,
who always tells me that I can
and believes in me until I do.

—————————

For all those striving to live big lives,
may you always have the courage to face your fears.

Introduction

Ifind it very interesting to be sitting here writing the introduction for a book that was not my inspiration to write. The fact that it's about inspiration is not lost on me either. This book is a testament to the fact that some of the greatest things we do in life will begin with a spark from without, not necessarily within. In my case, an acquaintance suggested I write a book, which left me laughing. When she insisted again more strongly, I was in stitches. But she wasn't joking. She asked me, "Don't you think you have wisdom to share?" After more than fifteen years of helping people break through their fears and limiting beliefs, and a lifetime of being burdened with and then breaking through my own, it was undeniable that I did. But the thought of taking that spark and igniting a full-blown fire was terrifying, which for me meant it was something that must be done. Within a week, I took on the challenge of writing this book.

I thought about the things I had overcome that had the greatest effect on my professional and personal life. I began getting a flood of memories of some of the thousands of other people's breakthroughs I have witnessed, and communications I received telling me about their impacts. Most importantly, I contemplated all the things I wish I had known about what was going on inside of my teenage brain, in regard to my fears, beliefs, and insecurities.

Writing this book was a new frontier in my work of inspirational speaking and the most fear-inducing experience of my life. Each chapter began with a blank page and even blanker mind. A weekly phone conversation with my book coach helped draw out some of the wisdom I had within me. I wrote a chapter a week at my home in Atlanta, always with the single flame of a candle as my writing companion.

Knowing what I want to write about and knowing what to write are two very different things. The fear that I might not know what to write, or have nothing to write, was constant and daunting at times. The only relief came when I was actually writing on my laptop, proving Ralph Waldo Emerson correct when he said, "Do what you fear, and the fear will die." By the last few chapters, near the end of the five-month-long process of writing, I felt truly alive.

"What does the reader need to know?" was a question I repeatedly asked myself. Keeping my focus on the reader helped the information flow. I was never at a loss for words once I conquered my fear, lit my candle, and began writing. As I wrote each chapter, it became clearer than ever that certain barriers to success are common to many of us—successful business leaders, college students, people in recovery, teenagers, and so on.

The aim of *Inspired Courage – Breaking Through Your Barriers to Success* is to help you understand that there is nothing "wrong" with you, and to take the mystery out of the inexplicable things within you that keep you from taking action. I hope the content of this book leaves you inspired to reach for new heights, and with the courage to take action to get there.

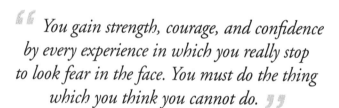

You gain strength, courage, and confidence by every experience in which you really stop to look fear in the face. You must do the thing which you think you cannot do.

— Eleanor Roosevelt
Former First Lady of the United States

CHAPTER ONE

What is Fear?

W^e can encounter many barriers to our success, and fear is one of our greatest. We've all experienced it—none of us is immune—but what is fear? In simplest terms, fear is an emotion, and with it can come intense physical sensations. Imagine driving home from work on a wintery night and suddenly losing control of your car on the icy road. Within a split second, you feel a range of emotions, from the anticipation of returning home, to surprise at the loss of control of your car, to full-blown terror faced with the possibility of serious injury or maybe even death. You feel your heart pounding out of your chest, adrenaline rushing through your body, and pins and needles in your hands, arms, and legs. Eventually your car comes to a stop, you catch your breath, do a quick mental inventory of the wellbeing of your body and car, and say to yourself something like, "Wow, that was a close call." What you just experienced is the human fight, flight, or freeze response. Most of us have experienced this at one time or another when faced with real *or imagined* physical danger. This fear keeps us safe by helping us avoid situations that might cause harm. And that's a good thing.

There are other times when we as humans are burdened with fear that can come in the form of an ongoing inner struggle rather than a single event. Unlike the fear designed to kick us into action to protect ourselves, this fear can paralyze us, leading to a cycle of self-doubt and inaction. As hard as we try, we can't seem to think this fear away. The more we try, the more powerful it gets, until we eventually give up on our pursuit of whatever it is we desire.

The inner struggle might look something like the following scenario: Steve is an employee at ACME Trucking Company. He has spent five years learning the ropes, working his way up from forklift operator, to shipping and receiving clerk, to his current position as inventory-control clerk. Steve's happy at his job and has excelled at every position he's held. Steve's boss mentions to him that there is an opening for inventory-control manager, and he should throw his hat in the ring. Initially, Steve's proud to be considered a worthy candidate, and he knows he could really use the pay increase that comes with the promotion.

As Steve daydreams about himself as inventory-control manager, he imagines all the ways the extra income will change his life. Maybe he can finally buy his first house. How exciting! Inexplicably, however, his excitement is replaced by a queasy feeling. Not sure what this is about, Steve is suddenly less excited about being a manager. He begins thinking that maybe he should stay in the job he's already familiar with. At least he's good at it. Besides, all the other managers have been at the company for ten years or longer, and they all have a college degree. After a few days of personal inner struggle, which he shares with no one, Steve decides it's best for him to stay put. He doesn't want to wear a tie to work anyway.

Fear is a dream killer! Fear of uncertainty and fear of failure just cost Steve his dream of being a manager and buying his first house. And it cost ACME Trucking Company the opportunity to promote from within, which would have been great for company morale. And while throwing in the towel may have alleviated Steve's fear, it burdens him with another inner tormenter, limiting beliefs.

When he quit on himself, Steve opened the door to a bombardment of inner criticism: "I'm not good enough," "I'm not smart enough," "I'm a coward," "I'm a failure," "I'll never amount to anything," "I'm a quitter," and the list goes on. While he may not be able to recognize what is happening in his mind, he can feel the toll this takes on his psyche. It's stressful and exhausting! I know, because I've lived it.

Confession, I am Steve. I am every Tom, Dick, and Harriet who ever let their fears and limiting beliefs get the best of them. This didn't happen because I'm a bad person or less deserving than others, no matter how much I might have thought that to be the case. It is just the way my brain developed. Like you, when I was born, my brain was a blank slate. Because of this, I was forced to look outside of myself for information on how to get my needs met and how to react and respond to situations. I recorded all this information in my little baby-brain operating system, adding programming with each new experience.

Unfortunately for me, I programmed myself with a lot of fear. My mom says that when I was a baby I would cry if someone even looked at me. I looked scared and on the brink of tears in many of my baby pictures. My two earliest memories from school are fear-based. My first memory is of being hysterical when my mom walked me to my classroom and left me alone with all those strangers. It didn't matter that they were little like me, they were strangers, and strangers to me were scary. I also remember having to perform the cancan dance in my elementary-school play. As a very shy tomboy, the prospect of dancing on stage in front of hundreds of strangers while wearing a dress was terrifying. I'd rather have gotten run over by the school bus. Luckily for me, on the morning of the play, I awoke with the mumps. Hallelujah, my prayers were answered!

A turning point in my childhood happened at nine years old during a Fourth of July parade in our small town of Davie, on the outskirts of Fort Lauderdale. A young girl was passing out flyers for our town's upcoming softball tryouts. This was exciting to me, and my first chance to play organized sports. And since my older sister and I would be on the same team, at least I wouldn't be alone, which for me meant "less scary." My brain was always on the lookout for something to be afraid of. What can I say? I was a weird, awkward kid.

As an athletic child, I excelled at sports and fell in love with softball. My speed and strong arm made me a natural infielder—shortstop and second base—with double plays being my favorite. I played on school teams and a summer travel team, where we won the Florida state championship when I was fifteen years old. I never felt more confident or courageous than when I was on the softball diamond. But for me, this confidence did not transfer to life outside of sports like it did for a lot of other kids. My deep-seated fear was too strong.

In my teenage years, I had plenty of friends and was an above-average student, but I lacked the confidence to take more advanced courses. Although older, I was still plagued by the fear and limiting beliefs of my early childhood. When we experience suffering for so long, it becomes a natural state of being. I missed many opportunities in my younger years because of my affliction.

As I grew into adulthood, I became less outwardly awkward and more adventurous, but I didn't outgrow this fearfulness and self-doubt. My entire existence was experienced through a thin filter of fear. Experiencing fear in this way affected every decision I made. It caused me to play life safe ... and small, without even realizing how it was restricting me.

By my early thirties, I was established in business and had experienced some success, in spite of this aspect of myself. After eight years of owning a small printing company in Miami, and holding positions in larger commercial print operations, I was now ready to transition to the world of advertising. I accepted the position of print-production director of a small boutique advertising agency in Coral Gables, Florida. I would be able to put the printing knowledge I gained over the previous twelve years to good use, while also learning a lot about the design process, strategy, and direct mail. It was a fast-paced environment, filled with impossible deadlines, fun creative types, and demanding clients from companies all over the country. Although the hours were long, I thrived working with some amazing people, who came together as a team to make what seemed like miracles happen on a daily basis. In my print/advertising career, this was as close as I had come to the rush of playing sports.

Sometimes life can change in unexpected ways. It just so happens that the two owners of the advertising agency I went to work for were big proponents of personal development, for themselves and their employees. They sent me to trainings and workshops that I would have never been exposed to, or even been interested in, had I not taken the job. To be honest, if I had been left to my own devices, I would have refused some of these opportunities, but since this was work related, I didn't want to limit my career or seem ungrateful. If they were willing to invest in me, the least I could do was show up.

Some of the experiences I had in these trainings had a profound effect on me. I was forced to look at the way I was moving through life and really connect my feelings with my actions or the lack thereof. I was beginning to understand my underlying feeling of fear and how it was limiting me in every area of my life.

I could no longer deny it. From the outside, it may have looked like I had it all together, but inside, I was a mess, and it was up to me to change that. I needed to understand why I had these fears and limiting beliefs in order to get myself out of this cycle of self-limitation. I set myself on a journey to understand what made me tick. As I began to change my orientation to fear and change my mindset, I became curious about what made others tick too. Why do we do the things we do, and maybe more importantly, what about those things we don't?

The more I learned about myself, the more courageous I became, to the point where I can now say that I am a woman who embraces fear. I compare this realization to lighting your home with electricity. Once you experience light in this form, you will never choose to go back to candlelight. It was a true awakening. When I look back at my life, I hardly recognize the person I was before this transformation. And I have to admit, if you told me in my late twenties that one day I would travel around the world, stand on stage in front of hundreds of strangers, and inspire them to overcome their fear, I would have told you "When pigs fly!" Not for a million dollars would I be able to do that.

Is there something you're afraid of? Whether you are someone like the younger me, who experienced fear in all aspects of life, like Steve who experienced fear when moving to the next level of success, or somewhere in between, change is possible for you. I am living proof of that.

If it seems too scary or too hard to change, or you often find yourself thinking, "Well, it's just the way I am. I'm not meant to be/have/do _____." (fill in the blank), I can assure you, it is not the case. That is your programming taking over, because that is what it does. Your programming is going to keep you doing what you've always done, until you make a conscious effort to change it. Keep in mind, if this is all new to you, you are moving through life with all your original programming. Now really, how successful can you expect to be with that kind of mindset?

Do you deserve to reach top-level success in your career, have a long-lasting, loving relationship, a healthy, energetic body, and so much more? Yes, of course you do. To do so, you will need to be willing to take risks, be vulnerable, move outside your comfort zone every now and then, but if your programming tells you it's not safe ... you aren't going to do it. Let me be clear, you are not your programming. You have the ability to change it, to make it work for you instead of against you, and it begins with taking the first step, which is becoming aware of what you want, and what is holding you back.

Let's look at how awareness could have helped our friend Steve at ACME Trucking Company. If Steve had become curious when that queasy feeling began, he might have become aware that it had to do with his job, or more specifically, the promotion. Self-discovery might have led Steve to recognize that maybe he had a fear of uncertainty, fear of failure, and possibly a limiting belief that he was not as smart as the other managers because he lacked a college degree. Steve might have also recognized that his boss wouldn't have encouraged him if he didn't believe he could do the job. Steve's boss actually believed in Steve more than Steve believed in himself. Steve also might have acknowledged that, since he'd learned to perform all those other jobs he excelled at, there was no reason he could not do so with this new one.

Unfortunately, Steve's programming determined that he had reached his highest level of success. He was now frozen in his comfort zone, unless he did something to override his existing programming, and essentially, created new programming. An upgrade, if you will. If he had done the personal work to become aware of all I just mentioned, he would then have been prepared to make a conscious decision on whether to stay in his current position until a later date or take action. Action would require courage and vulnerability. Steve could have expressed his concerns to his boss. Maybe his boss could allow him to spend a day or two shadowing the current inventory-control manager to see firsthand all that the job entailed. Another possibility is a little pep talk from his boss, telling him all the reasons he was a perfect fit. No matter how it turned out for Steve, having taken the step to becoming aware would have alleviated much of his fear ... so he could make his decision from a place of courage.

Is it time for you to finally break through one of your barriers to success by taking control of your programming, choosing to master your fear instead of letting it master you? Like me and Steve, you too have the ability to transform your fear into courage, looking within for your own inspired courage.

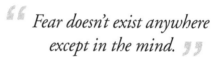

Fear doesn't exist anywhere
except in the mind.

— Dale Carnegie
American writer, lecturer

CHAPTER TWO

Fear and The Brain

Have you ever been afraid? Everyone has. I spend a lot of time speaking with people about fear in general and their personal fears specifically, and I have yet to meet anyone who has never had the experience of being scared. You may not realize it, but you've been facing and conquering fear your whole life and have overcome so many fears that you can't possibly remember them all. And just because you have had life-long experience overcoming fear, it doesn't mean there will come a time when you never feel fear again. Remember, fear is an emotion. Imagine committing to never feeling anger again. My guess is, even if you aced your anger-management course, you shouldn't be surprised to feel anger a time or two in the future. You are human after all.

While facilitating an event, I sometimes have the opportunity to ask a room full of adults to tell me what they are afraid of. I often hear common fears such as fear of public speaking, fear of spiders or other insects, fear of sharks, fear of heights, fear of strangers, fear of small spaces, fear of flying, fear of snakes, fear of clowns, fear of bad drivers, fear of hurricanes or other natural disasters, and of course, fear of fire. I have a lot of fun with this last one when facilitating a firewalk.

There are some more intense fears too, which don't usually get divulged until I ask them to go a little deeper and look for the fears that can really affect the quality of their life. Not surprisingly, we might not be as comfortable admitting these fears to others or ourselves. Often some of the following fears are confessed: fear of failure, fear of success, fear of success *and* failure (damned if you do and damned if you don't), fear of losing it all, fear of intimacy, fear of commitment, fear of losing house/home, fear of rejection, fear of being vulnerable, fear of being seen as weak, fear of not having enough money, fear of sickness or loss of a loved one, fear of death, fear of change, fear of being wrong or making mistakes, fear of not being qualified for a job, fear of never making enough money, fear of surgery, fear of being judged, fear of being embarrassed, and fear of being alone.

As you can imagine, we humans can carry a lot of fear. If you've lived long enough, you have seen the great lengths we go to in order to avoid feeling this unsettling emotion. Some fears are easier to avoid than others. Having lived most of my life in the Fort Lauderdale area, I grew up spending a lot of time swimming in the Atlantic Ocean. When the thriller motion picture *Jaws* was released, I avoided that film like the plague, because I knew that, if I saw it, I would never be able to enjoy swimming in the ocean again. If you have a fear of sharks, you are likely to stay out of the ocean. You can avoid snakes by staying out of the grass. Stay off ladders and rooftops, and you won't feel fear of heights. Fear circumvented and problem solved.

But some fears you avoid at your own peril. Avoiding fear of success may keep you from advancing in your career, which could cost you a lot of money over the course of your lifetime. Avoiding surgery could cost you your life. I have a friend who was terrified to have surgery. He recently found himself in the emergency room, experiencing shortness of breath. The doctor advised immediate open-heart surgery. My friend decided to wait and see if he could resolve his medical condition on his own, motivated by his emotional distress caused by his fear of surgery. A week later, he was rushed to the hospital by ambulance just in time for life-saving quadruple-bypass surgery. His fear that he would die in surgery did not come to fruition, and he actually handled the entire ordeal with courage and faith. This serves as proof that some of the things we fear, when faced, are not as scary as we imagined.

In *The Art of War,* Chinese general and philosopher Sun Tzu states, "If you know the enemy and know yourself, you need not fear the result of a hundred battles."[1] In the instance of battling our fear, the enemy lies within us; we and the enemy are one. Unlike the baby brain, which is required to look outside for information to survive, we must look within ourselves to conquer our enemy and thrive.

Before we engage the enemy, let's better understand it by taking a look at where it comes from.

We are born with very few fears, which means most of our fears are learned. So where do we learn fear? From the moment we are born, we learn fear from our parents, our caretakers, our culture, and life experiences.

Picture this. You're a little baby, six months old, and you're on the floor playing with your toys, and you're having a good time.

Into the room crawls an interesting-looking creature. It captures your attention. The interesting-looking creature comes towards you and crawls right up on to your arm. You've never seen anything like this before. Your little baby brain has no reference

---

1 Tzu, Sun (2019). *The Art of War* (p. 40). Garden City, New York: Ixia Press

point for it. You don't know what it is, but you're enjoying the sensation. You like this experience. This little creature is tickling your arm and leaving you giggling and loving it.

You're feeling a very positive emotion. Just then, your mommy walks into the room. Now, your mommy is terrified of spiders. She sees you on the floor with this big black spider crawling up your arm, and Mommy screams really loud. "AaaahhHHHH!"

Your mommy runs over to you, and then she swats the spider onto the floor, hitting you while doing that, and squashes your new furry friend with her foot. Next, she picks you up and says, "Did that big bad spider almost eat you up?"

So, what happened in your adorable little baby brain and body? Well, when you heard your mommy scream, it startled you. And when you saw the look on her face, the primal parts of your brain—the parts designed to keep you safe—kicked into action. In the simplest of terms, what you saw and what you heard sent a signal to your brain, specifically the thalamus, hypothalamus, and hippocampus, which all lead to your amygdala.

The amygdala, a small almond-shaped set of neurons located in your temporal lobe, is very powerful. It plays an extensive role in regulating your fear response.[2] It's responsible for sending out signals to the rest of the body that you are in danger. It's also responsible for recording that information in its database, so that the next time that situation arises, you know instantly that it means "Danger. Red alert."

So, in the seconds following your mommy's scream, your muscles contracted, your heart started beating faster, you started to perspire, and adrenaline and fifty other biochemicals pumped

---

2   Ressler, M.D., Ph.D., Kerry J. (2010). *Amygdala Activity, Fear and Anxiety: Modulation by Stress* (PMCID: PMC2882379). National Institutes of Health

into your little body, causing what we know as the fight, flight, or freeze response.

And, in addition to all this, the memory of this furry crawling little plaything became imprinted in your amygdala as something dangerous and to be avoided at all costs. One of the functions of the amygdala is to store the memories of things that we have, in our experience, perceived as dangerous. A friend of mine refers to the amygdala as "our little database of horrors."

From then on, every time we see, sense, smell, or experience that situation again, our body reacts to it with fight/flight/freeze.

And so now we have a human being that has been programmed to be afraid of spiders. You grow up and can't remember back to when you were six months old. All you know is that, whenever you see a spider, you don't feel so good; your muscles get tight, your heart races, and you're afraid of spiders.

This simplified example shows how quickly a human can be programmed, or conditioned, with fear. Your caretaker—your mommy in this instance—reacted to the spider based on her programming that spiders are dangerous, and sometimes even deadly. Had you not been in the room, your mommy's first reaction to seeing the spider might have been to flee: a flight response to her fear. But because her instinct to protect you was stronger than her instinct to protect herself, her brain kicked into gear with the fight response. Somewhere in your mommy's brain, she had programming that triggered her to put your safety above her own, and so she killed the spider. And had your mommy been an arachnologist, or been raised by one, her reaction probably would have been much different, based on different programming about spiders. Your mommy's reaction was well-intentioned, but it planted a seed about spiders that stuck.

Now that you know where fear comes from, it is probably unfair to consider it our enemy. Let's be honest, many of our fears served a purpose to keep us safe or under the control of others when we were younger. But now that we are older, the restrictions of some of these fears can cause real limitations in our life.

We are constantly reacting to situations based on our programming. Some programming keeps us safe, and other programming keeps us stuck, but we're not stuck with it.

I cannot overemphasize how my own life changed when I learned about the programming of fear. A year after the September 11 terrorist attacks in the United States, I had an opportunity to make a career change. It was not anything I had been planning, but like a lot of people during that time, I encountered drastic change in my industry. The busy advertising agency that I was employed by specialized in business-to-business and business-to-consumer direct mail. Anthrax attacks, intended to terrorize the media and members of Congress, were effective. Citizens were afraid to open their mail, and our clients put future investment in direct-mail campaigns on hold. What was once a growing agency, positioning itself for acquisition, was now going to close, taking the job I loved with it.

I took time and didn't rush into another job in printing or advertising. I was at a point in my life where my focus was turning from the pursuit of money and material things to one of greater fulfillment through contribution to society. I spent time traveling, visiting sacred sites in Peru, Europe, and the U.S., gaining an even deeper awareness of myself. I wanted to help others, but how? Firewalking! Of course! It makes perfect sense! Over time, I reflected on how my own firewalk experience had changed my perception of what is possible and transformed my limiting mindset. Three weeks on a spiritual journey through England,

Scotland, and Ireland confirmed that this was what I had to do: teach others to break through fear.

Tony Robbins was the only firewalker I knew, so I looked for the person who taught him to do it. He was just getting ready to retire, and I was able to twist his arm to do one more private training for me. As you can imagine, it was intense, and I broke through a lot of my own fears over those few days, but the teaching that had the greatest effect on me was learning that we are programmed with fear.

Even though I had been feeling more confident and courageous, I'd never wondered why I had these fears to begin with. It turns out I am not a victim of circumstance or bad thinking. Learning this was more liberating than my first firewalk, leaving me with a sense of freedom that money can't buy.

Over time, I trained myself to quickly recognize when I was feeling fear. I began to observe my feelings, physical and emotional, and my behavior. I got really good at noticing it very early on in the process. Instead of being paralyzed, I would recognize it and say to myself something like, "Okay, Connie, you're operating from fear here" or "Connie, you're not taking action because of fear." And next, I would ask myself a simple question: "Is this fear mine?" And the answer was almost always "No." I usually had no idea where the fear came from. If I hadn't fallen out of a tree or broken my arm falling off the bleachers in my past, why was I afraid to sit on the top row of the bleachers at the ballpark?

I started noticing and questioning the things that stimulated fear in me and observing my behavior, and it really changed my relationship with fear. It became much less threatening. And now I understood how my dad's white-knuckle drives across high bridges sent that fear of heights to everyone in the family. There was no reason for it, but it transmitted to me and my siblings, with lasting effect.

With some introspection, you can become aware of your own fears, and the obstacles that they create for you. You can begin your own practice to change your relationship with fear, with the ultimate goal of transforming your enemy (fear) into your helper (power).

The first step is to become aware of when you are feeling fear. Is there something you want to do but feel that fear blocks you? Does fear keep you from taking an action or make it hard or uncomfortable to take that action? Do you feel that you can't do something, or achieve what you want to achieve? As soon as you sense fear coming on, instead of pushing the feeling away, see if you can sit with it for a minute. Surrender to the feeling, and see if you can identify what it is. What is it fear of? This might be a little uncomfortable in the beginning, especially if you are accustomed to doing whatever is necessary to avoid feeling fear. If you have trouble identifying the specific fear, that's okay. You don't even need to know where it came from; chances are you won't anyway. Just training yourself to become aware of the fact that you are feeling fear is a big step towards self-awareness. Admitting that you are feeling fear is the most vital step to breaking through it!

Now that you're aware of your fear, a barrier to taking a specific action, you're ready for the next simple step. Ask yourself, "Is this fear mine?" If you're like me, the answer is almost always, "No, it's my programming." And even if you find that your answer is "Yes," the next action will be the same. Now that you're aware of what you're feeling and how it is limiting you, you are operating from an empowered position, rather than an emotional one, which is always the preferred state when making a decision. Now, what do you want to do about it? This is your fight/flight/freeze moment, and you get to choose your response!

Depending on your situation, you might decide that flight or freeze is the best response, waiting to tackle this another time. Maybe you need a little time to build up your courage to face your fear. There might be a more appropriate time to take action. As you learn to slow down your brain to make these decisions consciously, rather than reactively, you will improve your mindset.

If you choose to fight, meaning face your fear, you will now have the opportunity to change your programming. When you stand in the face of fear and take action anyway, you are changing your programming, no matter the result of your choice and action. Transformation comes from consciously moving through your fear, reprogramming your brain in the process.

From a very young age, as you responded predictably to the fears you were programmed with, you reinforced in your programming that, when you feel X, you will respond with Y. This is thanks to procedural learning—your memory system for learning habits and habitual functions. As your brain organized itself for survival, your body was developing patterns of response that became as automatic as the ability to ride a bike.[3]

From now on, think of your brain like Missouri—the "Show Me" state. Until you "show" your brain a new way to respond, it will keep giving you the same old subconscious programming. You'll need to harness the courage to disrupt the pattern of your programming. Every time you consciously take action to break through a fear, your brain is getting a new message towards action, instead of avoidance or paralysis. When you take action in a new

---

3   Fisher, Ph.D., Janina and Ogden, Ph.D., Pat (March 2011). *Retraining the Brain: Harnessing our Neuralplasticity.* Psychotherapy Networker (p. 3)

way, you are literally rewiring your brain, creating new neurons and neural networks.[4]

With practice, this can become a very quick process and eventually second nature. As you gain awareness and begin to question your fear, you'll see opportunities open up before you, and you may be surprised to see what you have the confidence to say "Yes!" to in the future.

---

4   Fisher, Ph.D., Janina and Ogden, Ph.D., Pat (March 2011). *Retraining the Brain: Harnessing our Neuralplasticity.* Psychotherapy Networker (p. 3-5)

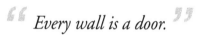

" *Every wall is a door.* "

— Ralph Waldo Emerson
American essayist, poet, philosopher

CHAPTER THREE

Opportunity Knocks

Opportunities appear throughout your life. Some go completely unnoticed and others are more obvious, leaving you with a choice to make. As you reflect back on your life, you might be able to pinpoint a series of precise opportunities, and how each one had a hand in leading you to where you are today. As a little girl, I was handed a flyer inviting me to a softball tryout, which led to playing competitive softball, travel, and eventually an athletic scholarship for college. Have you had experiences of serendipity that led you to great events or experiences that shaped your life? You might have had a job or two, friends, or maybe even a spouse who came into your life in this way. The beauty of life is that we never know where each twist and turn will lead us.

What would have happened if the girl who handed me that flyer had walked right past me? Would little nine-year-old Connie have chased her down to see what she was giving out? No, I never would have done that. It's impossible to know what would have come of my life had my parents not taken our family to the parade that day. The same can be said for every opportunity that we consciously choose to take a pass on or turn down. Sometimes we come to "no" clearly and easily, and other times it's "no" because "yes" is too darn scary. For some people, "no" is always the first and only answer, because "yes" could lead to change, and why in the world would we want that?

One of the biggest and most stressful changes we experience in life is changing jobs. When I took a new job as print-production director at an advertising agency, my job description and work environment changed drastically. I was always used to deadlines, but now they were coming from everywhere: clients demanding to see creative designs; printers, magazines, and newspapers waiting for artwork to meet their own production deadlines; and our creative team needing proofing changes to keep their work flowing. I learned fast and kept my focus on doing a great job.

Even with the extreme pressure of deadlines, this was the most positive work environment I had ever experienced. I realized early on that the two owners of the agency had done a lot of personal-development work to benefit themselves and the company. Whatever they had done must have worked, because their positivity was contagious, though not a feeling I was used to, especially at work.

My new bosses also invested in personal-development training for their employees, and early on in my job, it was my turn. A four-day training was coming to Orlando, and since I was the only new hire, I would be going alone. I said, "Yes," and then I was booked. Getting paid to be out of the office for four days—what a great perk! And then I found out I would be walking on fire on the very first night of the training. I didn't know what that was, but it really didn't sound like something I should be doing. Why in the world would someone do that? I was more than a little nervous and convinced my boss to go with me for the first night. It took quite a bit of arm twisting for her to be allowed to attend for one night only. Since her company had spent a lot of money with this training organization, they finally agreed for her to attend the first night with me. I was relieved, yet not feeling very positive about my upcoming training, and beginning to wonder if my new bosses were positively crazy!

The day had come to drive from Miami to Orlando for my training, which began on a Friday afternoon. I was conflicted about agreeing to the offer to attend. On one hand, the thought of doing something like walking barefoot across a bed of hot coals was far outside my comfort zone. Until I took this job, I had never even heard of such a thing. I had been secretly wondering if maybe I made a mistake. On the other hand, I was thrilled that my bosses thought enough of me to invest in my development, not just as an employee but as a person. I got a sense that they saw great value in what I was about to experience, so I decided to make the best of it and hide my apprehension as best I could.

Once at the convention center, we registered and waited to be allowed to enter the event space. I had no idea how many people there were, but it must have been more than three thousand. I looked around for any sign that I actually belonged there, and I noticed people of all ages, and every type of person you could imagine—businesspeople, couples, athletes, students, and probably just about every occupation was represented. I thought I'd fit in just fine. Doors finally opened and attendees rushed into the room and grabbed a seat. Rock music was blasting loud, and the energy was off the charts. People were on stage dancing, and so was the audience, some while standing on their chairs. I looked around, taking it all in. For an introvert, this was the beginning of a long four days.

For the next eight hours or so, the speaker was on stage, teaching us about getting into a peak state, anchoring, psychology, guided meditation, and a lot more. The atmosphere was akin to being at a rock concert, mega church, and magic show all at once. The only thing missing was a little person in a bright shiny outfit, juggling bowling pins. After many hours, I sensed we were nearing the time of the firewalk that I'd been dreading. I had mixed emotions at this point, feeling some pressure because my boss was sitting there beside me, but also knowing that I needed to be true to myself and follow my own freewill. By this point, the room was really getting amped up. The dancing and chant-shouting were becoming exhausting, but I guess they felt that was necessary to keep three thousand people from focusing on their fear.

We were going to leave the room now, but not to firewalk. We were being directed through the back of the building to see the fire as it burned down to hot coals for our firewalk in a few hours. I was shocked by how large it was. The bonfire was the size of a large house, and I could feel the heat from across the parking lot. People took turns getting as close as they could stand, to feel the intensity of the fire and hear the popping and crackling. I couldn't believe I was there!

Back in the room, there was no denying the decision I'd be faced with soon. I had seen the raging fire with my own eyes, and I couldn't escape the smell of smoke that I and three thousand others had brought back into the room. It just got real! I was both scared and excited for the challenge at the same time. For the next hour or so, I would dance, shout, create a power move to be used later, and work myself into a trance-like state as directed, all in the name of survival.

The time had come. Shoes and socks were off, and I walked again through the back of the building to the fire out in the parking lot, but this time we had to remain in our trance, which meant head facing up, staring at the sky, hands clapping, and shouting,

"Yes! Yes! Yes!" until it was our turn to walk. Seems easy enough, but I can assure you that, after fifteen to twenty minutes of this, you'd be willing to walk on fire just to get the pain in your neck to stop. My heart was racing, and I was filled with fear, as I imagined most of the others were as well, because everyone seemed to be following instructions to a tee.

The fire was different now, smaller and less fierce. Music was blaring, and I couldn't see much, not just because of the mass of people around me but mostly because I was too afraid to move my head down and take my eyes off the sky. I was following the person in front of me, who happened to be my boss. *Oh crap. Why did I make her come with me? In this crowd, it would be easy enough to disappear from the line and no one would be the wiser.* I kept inching towards the direction of my boss, looking up. "Yes! Yes! Yes!"

From what I could tell out of the corners of my eyes, there were many lines on either side of me, so people were walking one by one on the other fire paths at the same time, kind of like firewalker assembly lines. The atmosphere was filled with the fear of those waiting for their turn to firewalk and the excitement of those who had just stepped off the coal bed. Every few minutes, I'd hear the announcement, "Fresh coals!" which had a distinct way of getting my attention and gave me hope that maybe they wouldn't be so fresh when it was my turn.

In our trance-like state, we had inched our way to the front of our line, my fear building the closer we got. I heard them yell, "Fresh coals!" for our fire path, and I didn't need to look down to know that was not good news. My boss bravely went next, but I didn't dare watch; I knew only because of what I could hear. She must have survived, because I then found myself being guided up onto the sod. My chant then changed to "Cool moss," which I would continue to say out loud until I was safely off the fire.

The person in charge of my fire path excitedly told me, "Make your move!" This would be my power move, to trigger my anchor right before stepping onto the coal bed. I made my move and she told me, "You're ready! Go!" I took one step onto that coal bed and walked as quickly as I could to the other end. I was instructed to look up the entire time, so two people at the end had to stop me once I was off the fire path, and with that, I knew that I had done it! I had just walked barefoot across a bed of red-hot glowing embers! The feeling of accomplishment was indescribable. I couldn't really believe I did it! *I'm a firewalker!* I was then allowed to actually see what I did as I watched others firewalking and celebrating.

Eventually me and three thousand of my new closest friends walked barefoot back into the room and celebrated like our team had just won the Super Bowl, with each of us throwing or catching the game-winning pass. High fives and hugs everywhere. I was now deeply bonded with people who were complete strangers to me an hour prior. Going through a shared extreme experience gives us a knowing of what the other is made of and has been through. The sense of courage, bravery, and accomplishment in the room was palpable and set the stage for next three days. I was excited for the changes in me that were about to come.

For one of the first times in my life, I had a sense of the power that was within me. Getting myself to a point where I could still take action, even while filled with fear and self-doubt, was eye-opening for me. I learned that I don't have to be paralyzed by fear; often it will come down to a choice. Yes or no? Change or more of the same? Certainty or uncertainty? Stay stuck or grow? Adventure or boredom? Safety or calculated risk? I saw the power I have to create and shape my life with each decision I make.

The time spent before my actual walk across the coals was probably as informative as the firewalk itself. There was so much worrying and managing my emotional state, mainly because I was focused on what I thought was going to "happen to me" in the future, instead of the safety and fun I was actually experiencing in the moment. Interestingly, my firewalk was much simpler than I would have ever thought. Don't mistake that for being easy, because my mindset had not yet caught up to my ability. Physically it was simple, emotionally it was hard, or rather I made it hard on myself, but I suppose growth is like that.

My walk across the coal bed felt like I was walking on a warm pastry puff. The memory of that feeling has stayed with me, because it was so pleasantly unexpected. Today, walking into a bakery and seeing pastries can often bring back the memory of my first firewalk. And I remember the dime-size hot spot on the bottom of my foot fondly. It showed me that the fire was real, because without it, I would have sworn I must have walked beside the coal bed, not on it. Remember, it was drilled into my head to keep looking up. That tiny red spot and slight burning sensation, the trophy I attained for using my courage, would be with me until I fell blissfully to sleep that night. By morning, the spot was totally gone, and I would marvel at how quickly we heal and grow.

You never know how, and when, the opportunities that come your way will impact your life. If you did know, I think it would not only clarify your decisions but also, on occasion, impede your growth. For me, if I had known that taking a new job would lead to a firewalk, which years later would lead me to being on stage in front of large audiences, helping them break through their fears, I would never have taken the job. It was out of my realm of possibility. Luckily, life doesn't give us the whole game plan. All you can do is have faith that you are making sound decisions and then hold on for the ride.

I would like to think bosses aren't making a habit of setting their employees up to fail. I'm pretty certain my new bosses would not have spent the time or the money to send me to a training where they thought I would have been physically or emotionally harmed. A good boss recognizes the potential and what will aid in the development of each specific person. Some opportunities will come to you when you are ready, which at times might lead to thinking you are not being treated fairly, if things aren't happening soon enough to fit your timeline. It's not about everything being equal; it's about what a person needs at the time and what will help them develop, setting people up for success when the time is right. If you feel strongly that you are ready for a new opportunity or challenge, take a step by letting the decision maker know of your interest. Then you know that you did all you could in that circumstance.

Whether or not to accept an opportunity or challenge in life is only the first part of the equation. The second part is what type of mindset you bring to the challenge. This is where your programming comes in. Even though my fearful programming was my travel companion, not just to Orlando but everywhere, I decided before my training even started that I was going to make the best of it. I was going to learn all I could, whether I walked on fire or not. This mindset left me open to learning the most valuable lesson from the training, which for me was that I had within me the ability to take action every time I face fear. This led to a gradual change in my programming, to embracing fear rather than running from it. What kind of mindset are you bringing to your workplace, your relationship, your parenting, or your future? Is your mindset leading you to growth or hindering it?

As you grow throughout your life, in all areas of life, it's important to stay true to yourself. Picture yourself at the firewalk. Your growth would have come from you being able to make decisions for yourself, harnessing your courage to overcome your own programming as you stood before the fire. There is no value in you feeling coerced or pressured to do something like this, whether or not you felt ready for it. This could lead you to feeling victimized, instead of empowered, and could lead you to lose confidence in yourself and those who sent you there. As you can see, this would set you up for a very negative experience and possibly an injury.

To this day, I still feel a deep sense of gratitude for my first firewalk experience. Someone taking a chance on me, and me having the courage to take a chance on myself, would change my life for the better. After years of learning to face and eventually embrace my fears, I have come to teach others to empower themselves through firewalking and other breakthrough activities. I have learned that it doesn't take eight hours of trance, meditation, or "ra-ra" to be able to transform your mindset. I have grown to have faith that each person can face that fire themselves, choosing when they are ready to take that first step into the fire, rather than someone else telling them they are ready. There is real value in them making a conscious decision to take action in the face of fear and self-doubt, because this isn't about the fire at all. It's about using the energy and the empowerment from a night of firewalking to propel you to success in your future.

The purpose of this book is to share all I have learned in changing myself to inspire others to make changes for themselves. I am humbled when I think of the thousands of people who have faithfully followed me to their breakthrough experience, bringing what's on the inside to the outside. I take no credit for what they accomplish; I merely provide the opportunity, or the space, for them to create it for themselves. And the thing I hear most often is this: "That was so easy!" It can be for you too, if you have the curiosity to know what's knocking, and the courage to say, "Yes!" Opportunity knocks ... but it's up to you to open the door!

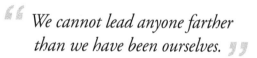

We cannot lead anyone farther than we have been ourselves.

— John C. Maxwell
American author, speaker, pastor

CHAPTER FOUR

Leaders Go First

In his final speech, Vince Lombardi said, "Leaders aren't born; they are made. And they are made just like anything else, through hard work. And that's the price we'll have to pay to achieve that goal, or any goal."

Okay, working hard makes sense to become good at anything, but what other characteristics are leaders made of? Any of the following long list of characteristics probably come to mind: passion, clarity, decisiveness, honesty, responsibility, humility, authenticity, accountability, vision, confidence, commitment, enthusiasm, empathy, courage, communication, positivity, creativity, motivation, determination. But the one thing—the most vital thing—any leader must have is followers, and that is where the true test of leadership comes in.

When a leader of a company or organization hires me to speak and facilitate breakthrough activities, I already know I am dealing with a leader with a vision, who wants to empower and inspire their team. What I don't know, at this point, is how the team will respond to their leader's challenge. But I suppose the leader already has a good sense of this because of what happens every day in their workplace. The leader is setting goals, creating new initiatives, and making changes for greater productivity and success, and they know how their team will respond to the never-ending challenges.

I have sat across the desk from leaders lacking vision, who have told me some version of the following: "Board breaking looks great for their people, but mine could never do that." I've often wondered what it must be like to work for someone who has such a low opinion of the people they lead—the people who are vital to successfully carrying out the mission. It is possible their apprehension is a testament of their lack of ability to lead, rather than their team's ability to follow. In this instance, it appears the leader is the one in need of a little inspiration and possibly a breakthrough or two.

In defense of the type of leader mentioned above, there is a common occurrence that most people are not aware of. We each have our own programming, and when we don't keep it in check, we can unknowingly put our limitations onto others. If we are not self-aware, we can project our own fears onto others and presume everyone has the same limitations. Leaders will be tested to be on the lookout for this propensity.

My true leadership test came when I transitioned to a new career, one so different from my previous one that I would be required to rely on traits that were not yet my strengths. Where I once worked one-on-one with a designer or printer to produce a tangible printed product, I was now going to stand in front of groups of people and help them build something intangible, yet so much more important: confidence, courage, and self-esteem. In business, I had the opportunity to manage others, and I was about to come face to face with the difference between managing and leading. I now had my first client, and I was going to facilitate my very first firewalk. Exciting, and yet scary at the same time. The leader of a personal-development organization was entrusting me to guide her members through what she wanted to be a life-changing experience, and I had no room for error. I had to get this right.

The date was set! New Year's Eve and the organizer wanted the participants to be walking barefoot across a bed of red-hot coals at the stroke of midnight—literally taking a quantum leap from one year into the next. And if that was not enough pressure for me, she wanted me to pull out all the stops to give her folks a night they would never forget. In addition to the firewalk, they would be breaking boards with their bare hands, breaking arrows and bending steel rebar with the soft part of their throats, and walking barefoot across broken glass. And let me remind you, this was my very first event! I had no idea how long it is going to take to facilitate those activities and get these people out to the fire and ready to walk at midnight. And even if I did know how long it would take, I was not only managing this event but I was the leader. Would I have what it takes to get them to follow me through this process of transformation?

As I was going through the planning process, I realized that it had been seven years since my very first personal firewalk experience. Since then, I had firewalked many times, along with other adventurous and consciousness-raising experiences, so many that sometimes I hardly recognized the person I used to be. Maybe you have an area of life where you have grown so much that it is difficult to remember your old way of being. If I was going to lead these people through their fears, it was important for me to get in touch with mine, to remember what they would be feeling in the moment they faced each challenge. I could remember that I was scared standing in front of the fire for my very first firewalk, but I wanted to feel that fear again. I needed to feel the intensity of that emotion, and the self-doubt that often comes along with it.

Skydiving would do the trick! Not only had I never gone skydiving before, but the thought of it was so frightening that I had a premonition I would probably have a heart attack if I ever attempted it. There was no denying it. If I was going to be an authentic leader, I would need to put on my big-girl panties and parachute, and then take the plunge. (More on skydiving in the next chapter.)

After skydiving, I knew I could facilitate my first firewalk event with confidence. I needed that jump from the plane to put me in the right mindset to inspire others to break through their fear. Good leaders are continuously exemplifying the behaviors they would like from their team members, and I wanted to be congruent in my leadership and teaching. I believe courage is contagious, as is fear, and the most important thing for the participants to sense is that I had learned to embrace fear, and that they could do the same. Leaders set the stage by going first.

On New Year's Eve, my team and I facilitated our very first firewalk experience, along with all the other activities, myself going first at each turn. I found that I was able to lead others, and with the participants having trust in their organization's leader, faith in me, and a willingness to face their fear. Each and every one of them voluntarily and courageously completed each challenge, and we found ourselves walking across the red glowing embers at midnight. As fireworks filled the night sky, the fire filled us with anticipation for what was to come in the new year.

You might wonder why in the world I would do something like skydive, if I thought I could harm myself doing it. Well, the truth is, the thought of standing in front of a group of strangers feeling like a fraud was more terrifying than the thought of jumping out of an airplane. For me to believe I could inspire and empower others, I needed to do the same for myself. Personally, in this instance, skydiving worked. I wanted to have that experience of skydiving so they could relate to me, and I could relate to them. It put me in a position where I could accurately describe what they were feeling and actually encourage them to take those first steps, which are so important in achieving anything. I wanted to be able to anticipate their needs and their feelings, so that I could help them work through it, encourage them properly, and help them learn as much as they could about themselves in the short time we had together. I put their needs before my own, which is what good leaders do.

It is important to note here that I did not tell the participants that I went skydiving. This was a personal experience to push myself past my limits, which I was then going to use to help them do the same for themselves. When we change on this level, we don't need to go around telling people what we did; it will be conveyed in how we carry ourselves and by our actions. I'm sure you know someone who is always out to prove that, whatever you accomplished, they did it too, just more of it, and faster and better than you. I was never going to stand in front of a group and say, "I went skydiving, so you should be able to this!" Would you feel comfortable following a leader, one who thinks they're better than everyone else, into the fire?

As you can see, it's so important for a leader to influence and encourage rather than command. If you are in a position of authority, you might be able to order people around, and they might actually do what you say for a little while, but it will be out of respect for the position you hold, rather than respect for you. People don't follow authority. This kind of leadership will only get you so far.

I have found a little humility as a leader can go a long way. If you've read this far into my book, you know by now that I do not proclaim myself to be a fearless person. Being fearful and acknowledging it has helped me when I have needed to break through fear. Admitting that I am this way helps build the trust of others, so that I can lead them and teach them all that I have learned to help them cross the fire, not just to become firewalkers but to go on to accomplish much bigger things.

A similarity that I've noticed with most of the leaders I've had the privilege to work with is that they ask me if they can go first. Whether it is board breaking or firewalking, they want to be the first to go, right after my demonstration. I always admire this willingness to be vulnerable, risking failure in front of their team. Even standing in the face of fear, and the self-doubt that often accompanies it, they have the courage to take the lead. Leaders go first. And on a few occasions, I have seen something extraordinary: A leader willing to give up the spotlight when a team member expresses a desire to face their fears and go first. A leader actually letting an aspiring leader take the spotlight and go first. A win/win/win for all involved: the leader, the aspiring leader, and all those able to witness this act of confident leadership.

Throughout our lifetime, we have had many opportunities to be in the position of leader and follower. When we are young, we can unknowingly change the trajectory of our life with the choices we make about who to follow and why. Some childhood leaders reveled in bringing out the worst in us, wanting company for their shenanigans. Perhaps *we* were the leader in the mischief a time or two.

We could be attracted to other leaders because they bring out the best in us. I was blessed to have great softball coaches, beginning with my dad. I had an excellent coach for my thirteen to fifteen-year-old summer travel team. He selected the best players and put us in the most appropriate positions to match our talent. He was able to get each of us to give 110 percent effort in the pursuit of being the best, and one summer we did just that, winning the state championship. Nothing brings a team together like success, whether it's playing sports or in the workplace.

Whether you are an existing leader, an emerging leader, or someone who has not yet given thought to becoming a leader, reflect back on any good leaders you've had in your lifetime. Don't limit yourself to the workplace or your career. Think about teachers who might have been able to persuade you to try a little harder. Maybe a parent or relative you went to for guidance for a specific issue or during a difficult period in your development. Maybe a mentor who helped you further your career or education. Which characteristics did you find most drew you to this leader? Any characteristics that you most admired? If you are currently a leader, are there any characteristics that were so influential that you have modeled your own leadership style after them?

Why did you follow the leaders you did? Was it the honesty and tough love they gave you to persuade you from making a big mistake in a career decision? Did you feel this leader always had your best interest in mind? Maybe they were unselfish in the time and guidance they gave you. How about a leader that actually shared some of the pitfalls they encountered, and mistakes they have made, in order to teach you the ropes? Can you see the value in having a humble leader like this? What did your leaders teach you? Why did you respect them?

If you are a leader, how do you get others to follow your leadership? Are there some areas where you know you can improve? Can your people relate to you, and just as importantly, can you relate to them? Are you congruent in modeling the behavior that you are seeking from them? What mindset do you bring to work every day? Do you embrace change or resist it? Ultimately, your role as a leader is to create the next generation of leaders, ensure a seamless transition, and continue the growth of your organization as even bigger successes develop. And the greatest compliment you can have as a leader is developing someone that reaches a higher potential.

Leadership guru John C. Maxwell says, "A leader is one who knows the way, goes the way, and shows the way." What kind of leader are you or do you aspire to be? Do you have the courage to lead? The coals are glowing.... Leaders go first!

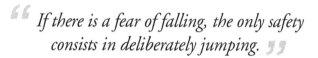

If there is a fear of falling, the only safety consists in deliberately jumping.

— Carl Jung
Swiss psychiatrist, psychoanalyst

CHAPTER FIVE

Jump

Now, on to my skydiving adventure! I mentioned earlier that I was seeking a way to replicate the fear that I experienced standing in front of the bed of glowing red-hot coals at my very first firewalk. I felt the need to put myself through a personal test, to see if I had it in me to practice what I preach about breaking through fear. If I am going to stand in front of a group and tell them that they can gain confidence and build courage by pushing their limits, I needed to prove to myself that I could do the same. Skydiving would be my test, but I didn't come to this decision lightly. I admire people who have skydiving on their bucket list, but it was conspicuously absent from mine. Not surprisingly, since I thought the experience would scare the life right out of me with a heart attack. Skydiving was so far over the edge of my comfort zone that I viewed it as something that would either kill me or make me stronger and better on every level.

Skydiving may sound like a drastic choice, but this is how important it was to me. I was about to embark on a new career, one where I would have to acquire a whole new set of skills. I never had to influence or encourage a printing press to give me a darker shade of red. Just punch a few buttons and voila! I had a sneaking suspicion it was going to take some pretty inspiring language to convince strangers to follow me barefoot across a bed of hot coals. For an introvert who suffered from shyness early in life, this was going to be a tall order, and I needed a sign that I was not suffering from delusional thinking.

I was approaching my fortieth birthday, and less than thirty days later, I would be officially kicking off my new career with a New Year's Eve firewalk. As you can imagine, this was a very exciting time in my life. I found myself in the midst of party-planning *and* planning my first empowerment event. It was vital that I put myself through my personal test of skydiving before New Year's Eve, and time was running out. What better time than a milestone birthday to achieve a remarkable feat. December third it is!

Have you ever had a great idea, and then by the time ten of your closest friends and relatives give you their unsolicited opinion, you are left feeling demoralized and defeated? Me too, which is why I couldn't risk telling anyone about my desire to test my mettle with skydiving. I had a short window to make it happen, and the last thing I needed was to be swayed by the fear of others. A friend once told me to share my dreams only with people who could help me reach them. I had no choice. I had to make a plan and keep it under wraps.

It's not easy to keep something from your partner, especially when it involves voluntarily putting your life at risk. All good relationships and partnerships are built on trust, and what I really needed right then was for her to trust me to make this big decision. I realized I could not sneak out of the house and disappear for an extended period and not risk destroying trust built over the past eight years. In my most serious tone, I said, "Karen, I am going to leave for a few hours, very early Saturday morning. Please trust me and promise you won't ask any questions." She agreed, and I have to confess, I did have fun over the next few days, watching her bite her tongue to keep her promise.

Everyone should have at least one friend who really gets them and would do anything for them, and for me, it is my dear friend John. We've been through countless exciting times and adventures together. He's the Thelma to my Louise. "Meet me at a parking lot a mile from my house Saturday morning at seven a.m. Don't ask any questions. I'll fill you in later." He agreed to my plan. Saturday came, and I told him we were heading to Homestead. Excited to guess what was going on, he asked if I was going to ride with a NASCAR driver. Nope, already did that.

"You're going skydiving!" he yelled.

Yes. Yes, I am. And with that, John was all in!

I still remember this day like it was yesterday. The conversation on the hour-long drive to the airport was light and fun, as it always was with John. On the inside though, I was in deep reflection about what I was about to do. I am not a daredevil, and I wasn't going to just jump out of a plane for no reason. I had prayed about this, and I was looking for a sign that I was heading down the right path. This jump for me represented jumping into a new life, one filled with uncertainty, and I had faith that this jump would give me a clear answer. I had to surrendered to the experience with no attachment to the outcome.

In case you are wondering if I had a death wish, I did not. Up to this point, I was as content as I had been in my entire life. I was very happily married, my family was healthy, and I was traveling a lot. I was just a woman in need of confirmation. I was thoughtful in my planning, knowing that family and friends would be at my house later, so if I were to perish, there would be a support network, with all the people I loved (and who loved me) together.

It would fall on John to deliver the news that I died doing what I loved, and I knew he would do that for me.

After arrival, it would be hours before I took my leap of faith. I first had to sign seven forms, each containing legal jargon to convey the fact that skydiving is dangerous, and that people die doing it. With John standing over my shoulder, I signed each form and braced myself for the fear to set in. Now on to the jump selection. There are three altitudes to jump from, so I choose the lowest one at 8,000 feet. This was already so far out of my comfort zone that I didn't need to jump from 13,500 feet. The clerk told me that the one I selected would be too short, over before I knew it, which sounded great to me. She and John encouraged me to jump from the height of 11,000 feet. Suddenly, I was feeling brave.

I got fitted for my very unflattering jumpsuit and harness, resigned that I would look like a blue marshmallow falling from the sky. There were a lot of laughs as I met others taking their first jump that day too. I hadn't begun feeling fearful yet, but I figured I would when the time got closer. I was paying close attention to my emotions, so that—for the sake of those I would later teach—I could get in touch with what they were going to feel facing their fear.

I met Greg, a tall redheaded man who would be my tandem partner. He had made thousands of jumps and seemed to love his job. He taught me everything I needed to know, and when the plane was ready, we were strapped together so tightly that I could feel his every breath on my back. We climbed into a little fifteen-seater prop plane, which is not easy with a six-foot-tall man strapped to your back. I was pretty sure I was going to be feeling fear when the engine fired up on the plane.

There were twelve of us sitting quietly on the floor of the little plane. I could tell from their gear that most were avid skydivers.

After about twenty minutes, we leveled off and the pilot announced, "Good news! We're all dropping from 13,500 feet!" *What? Wait a minute! I didn't sign up for this!* I had been feeling brave at my mid-level altitude of 11,000 feet. Apparently, they couldn't read minds, because the next thing I knew, they were rolling up the side door and jumpers were lining up, experienced jumpers going first. One by one, they dove out the door, and within a second, each one transformed from a human standing in the doorway to a small speck of pepper in the brilliant blue sky. And the most amazing thing was the sound as they left the plane: *Shoop. Shoop. Shoop. Shoop. Shoop.* Mere seconds in between each skydiver, and now it was my turn. I was surprised at how calm I was, but certainly I was going to lose it when I got to the door. Greg and I crawled over to the door on our knees, and I was looking out, taking in the view. He told me we were jumping on three. I felt myself smiling. "One ... two ... three (JUMP)!"

For some reason, I took in a deep breath on "two," as if I was jumping into a swimming pool, which meant my lungs were full of air as we freefell for sixty seconds at 120 mph. The feeling of freefall is amazing, like being a human bullet, and the air rushing past me was deafening, which is why experienced skydivers use hand signals. I was trying to get Greg's attention to let him know I couldn't breathe. He yelled for me to inhale. I was, and I still couldn't breathe! If you want to know what it felt like, take in a big deep breath, and for the next sixty seconds try to take in more air without exhaling, and imagine you are flying through the air at 120 mph.

When my altimeter read six thousand feet, I could finally pull the cord. The parachute opened and our momentum stopped with such force that my legs swung from behind me in my prone position to up in front of my head. The force pushed the air from my lungs, and I could *finally* breathe. In my freefall, I needed to exhale, not inhale! From this vantage point, I was floating like a bird, and I could spot landmarks as far as Miami Beach and the Florida Keys. I could see traffic and farm equipment moving, but I couldn't hear a thing—stillness like I had never felt before. I was at peace and my heart was full. I could appreciate the vision of birds of prey, and also big-vision people who don't get too wrapped up in the little details. I got ten glorious minutes to take it all in and think about my next forty years as we floated back down to the ground.

After a safe landing in the drop zone, unharnessed from Greg, I looked up to the heavens, fell to my knees, and kissed the ground, grateful for my sign that I was heading down the right path. And standing there was John, a partner in so many of my adventures, smiling from ear to ear. He looked proud of me, as I was of myself. He didn't know it, but I was now free from my burden of doubt about whether I could pull off my second act. I was now looking forward to our New Year's Eve firewalk.

As I got closer to home, I was still feeling great about my accomplishment, but I was starting to feel a little uneasy about how my late arrival would be received. I was hours later than I anticipated and feeling a bit guilty that my parents were now helping Karen get ready for my party. It is funny how, no matter how old we get, some of us are still afraid to disappoint our parents. Chalk that up to our programming too. I was greeted with "Where were you? You're late." I showed them my skydiving certificate, and they were in disbelief. No one was mad, but my mom was slightly disappointed that she didn't know, because she would have jumped too. I didn't see that coming!

To say this had been a surprising day would be an understatement. It was a day filled with the unexpected. The fear that I was preparing myself for from the moment I awoke never came. The universe, not letting me play it safe, had the pilot drop me from 13,500 feet. I mistakenly thought I needed to relive that feeling of fear, but what I really needed to remember was what I felt like in the moments immediately *after* my first firewalk, not before. What power there is in realizing that what we fear often never appears! We don't have to live with the fear of fear.

How many times have you anticipated fear that never materialized? Have you ever done anything like I did to myself with skydiving? I spent half a day certain that fear was just around the corner. Why is it so easy for us to have unrealistic expectations of what will scare us, or worse, that we won't be able to handle the fear if it occurs? Why could I not have expected being fearless going skydiving? I had spent the last seven years doing all kinds of things to help me grow in this area. Skydiving proved to me that the more we consciously and intentionally face fear, and take action in the face of fear, the less often we will feel fear. Maybe this is why some of our fearful experiences never materialize. Is it possible we have grown in certain areas and not yet recognized our growth?

Our fears can often be unrealistic and unreasonable. We need to remind ourselves that fear is an emotion. How many other emotions are we expending so much energy to predict and avoid? Humans are very poor at predicting how we're going to feel in the future, and yet we keep doing it with fear. This behavior can sap the joy out of life. Maybe in some of these instances, when you are predicting fear, you might want to remind yourself that the very opposite could be the case. Realize you may never feel the fear you're bracing for. No need to be fearful of a fear that might never come.

Years ago, I had my first surgery. My existing mindset left me worried that my fear would be overwhelming, so I made a deal with myself. I gave myself permission to feel fear, but it had to be because there was actually something to be afraid of in that moment. I was in the hospital for two days, and the staff was so caring and explained everything that was going to happen so well that I never got scared, and I never felt pain. Now, being in the hospital is not an enjoyable situation, but why create a bunch of fear that is guaranteed to make it worse?

Are there moments in your life you know would be much more enjoyable, or maybe where your performance could improve greatly, if you could just live in the moment? This is called "being present," and the simple practice of mindfulness can help you make this a more natural state of being. The easiest and most accessible way to bring yourself back to the here and now is to breathe. Breath is a fantastic tool, and you can't go anywhere without it! As soon as you notice you have begun worrying about the future, feel anxious, or sense your thoughts are taking you in a direction you don't want to go, focus on your breath. Focusing on each breath in, and each breath out, repeat to yourself, "I am here now. I am okay. I am safe."

If you want a challenge to help build your mindfulness muscle, do something like focusing on your right hand every minute of every day for a week! Again, it's easily accessible and no one knows you're doing it. While it is impossible to accomplish this for every single minute of a day, you'll be amazed at how you improve from day one to day seven. Your mindfulness practice will help you realize how often random thoughts can take control of you. Remember, you are not your thoughts, and you can direct your thoughts. Where focus goes, energy flows. You can decide to put your energy into your present, rather than your past and your future.

If you've ever spent time with a great salesperson, you probably noticed they possess some characteristics lacking in unsuccessful salespeople. A new or not-yet-successful salesperson is focused on the reply—in most cases the rejection—before they ever pick up the phone. They're already predicting what the response will be and their emotion attached to it. A great salesperson doesn't take anything personally and has learned that fear of rejection is unreasonable, because rejection is part of their job. Over time, they have mastered that fear and have no trouble picking up the phone to make the call and ask for the sale.

The same is true for relationships. How many great relationships never happened because someone was too afraid to take a chance, fearing what the response might be? If you can relate to any of this, it's not too late. Pick an area you want to grow in and commit to being courageous in the face of your fear until you master it. Just remember to breathe—inhale *and* exhale.

Now it's your turn: One … two … three (JUMP)!

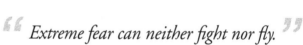

Extreme fear can neither fight nor fly.

— William Shakespeare
English playwright, poet, actor

CHAPTER SIX

F#*K Everything And Run

What we fear takes different forms. Some of us fear heights and others will not be bothered by heights at all. I always marvel at people who can walk along steel beams as they build skyscrapers, or window washers on those tall buildings who dangle from ropes, swinging themselves wildly from side to side as they clean. Some people will let the sight of an insect keep them from entering a room. A close encounter with a dog, usually man's best friend, can strike fear in some. Other people's fear of dentists can be so strong that they can't even stand to meet one in a social situation.

We all have fears, and obviously we won't all have the same set of fears, but what matters more than the fears we have is how we react to them. Some of our fears might not limit us at all. If you have a fear of heights and never have to climb a ladder to paint, change a lightbulb, or enter an attic, it probably won't affect your quality of life the slightest bit. But how would you react if your three-story office building had a fire on the first floor? Perhaps by the time the fire department arrives, everyone is anxious but safe on the third floor, and you're relieved to see the bright-red hook and ladder truck arriving at the scene. Within minutes, these brave firefighters have their ladder in position to start evacuation, picking you to go first. They are going to guide you out the window onto their long ladder, climbing with you down to safety. How would you react?

I've spent years getting to watch people up close as they react to their fears. Although some of the activities I use stimulate fear, it is not just for the sake of scaring people. I would consider it purposeful fear. I am helping people go through their process of fear, so that they can become aware of what they feel, what they do, and how it limits them, and give them a chance to learn to break through their fear so they can accomplish their goals. I like to keep things easy and memorable, and what better way than using an acronym? We have become accustomed to acronyms for everything. Getting a visit from the I.R.S. or F.B.I. can really stimulate fear in us, so why not an acronym about fear?

At speaking engagements, I will often ask people to tell me what the acronym F.E.A.R. stands for. Depending on the specific group or situation, I hear different answers. An addiction recovery group might say F.E.A.R. means "Face Everything And Recover" or "Few Ever Arrive Rejoicing." Sometimes I hear funny things like F.E.A.R. means "Forget Everything And Relax" and "Forget Everything And Remember." From the military, "Force Elements At Readiness." From positive people, I might hear "Face Everything And Rise" or "Forgetting Everything's All Right." And don't worry, there's one from you pessimists too, "Future Events Already Ruined."

For the sake of my teaching, F.E.A.R. stands for "False Evidence Appearing Real," and many people are already familiar with this one. Fear is an intense emotion, and when we're in it, it has a way of amplifying other thoughts and feelings, helping to make things that aren't true feel very real, especially in regards to our perceived limitations.

One of my favorites, usually heard at a firewalk after the group has seen that the fire has been lit, is that F.E.A.R. stands for "F#*k Everything And Run," or the G-rated version, "Forget Everything And Run." This always gets a huge laugh and lets me know that they are aware of what's coming. The fire has been lit, and short of their prayers for rain being answered, we will soon be walking on fire. For them, this just got real! During this time, the mood in the room often changes, and I see people taking things a little more seriously. From the looks on their faces, I can tell that some are sitting in serious self-doubt about their ability, probably wondering, *What in the world have I gotten myself into?* And some even look like they wish they could F#*k Everything And Run!

If you have ever had the experience of being in over your head, you can relate to this. I wish I could tell you that F#*k Everything And Run is always an option, but it's not. If this were the case, this would be a very short book. Sometimes we get ourselves (or life puts us) into situations where we're forced to break through our fear, because we have no other choice, and this book is designed to help you do just that.

I'm now going to take you on one of my "in over my head" adventures. Having grown up in South Florida, I had no exposure to mountain ranges until my early twenties, when I became a recreational snow skier. On one particular trip, my friend Patty and I flew to Breckenridge, Colorado, for a week of skiing. I looked forward to these once or twice-yearly vacations and skied from the time the lifts opened until they closed to take advantage of every minute on the slopes. At this point, I was an intermediate skier, meaning I felt pretty confident on beginner and intermediate trails, and hadn't spent much time on the expert trails.

Ski resorts do a great job at marking the trails with signs, so skiers can make choices based on their own ability, in an effort to keep skiers safe. Each trail sign has a shape and color: green circle is easiest, blue square is difficult, black diamond is more difficult, and double black diamond is most difficult. These are also referred to as beginner, intermediate, expert, and expert only. Trail names will give you a clue to the level of difficulty too. A name like Red Rover sounds very pleasant, and it's a green beginner trail. Purgatory and Hades? If you guessed double black diamond, you are correct. Skiers also carry a color trail map, so they can navigate based on their ability and see a bird's eye view of all the mountain trails and where they lead.

Once we were in Breckenridge, we met up with Patty's friend CiCi and spent our vacation skiing together. CiCi was an expert skier who grew up skiing with her sister, who was on the U.S. Olympic ski team, so obviously Patty and I were way out of our league skiing with her. Toward the middle of our trip, we decided to take turns leading the others for the day. The leader called the trails, and wherever she went, the others followed. Patty loved skiing through the trees, so we did that for her day. Mogul trails are my favorite, with big bumps requiring a lot of turns and quick planning a few turns ahead. If you miss a turn or two, it's easy to find yourself airborne.

On CiCi's day, she wanted to ski Copper Mountain, only a thirty-minute drive away. CiCi led us all over Cooper Mountain, and she had only one speed: fast. She was hard to keep up with, and you can't let your friends get too far out of your sight while skiing or you'll spend the rest of your day trying to find them. Most of the day was spent skiing black-diamond trails that I never would have taken if I were calling the shots. It was a rush skiing so fast and getting to so many places where there was no turning back. I could feel myself improving as the day went on.

After lunch, CiCi decided we were going to ski Spaulding Bowl, which is on Copper Mountain's highest peak. I had never skied a bowl before, and would never have considered it, but I did commit to follow her lead, so off we went. After a long chairlift ride, I was getting nervous, but we were not there yet. I now had to take a T-bar lift called Storm King to the peak. There were no chairs on this lift. I had to put a metal bar shaped like a big T behind my legs and let the rope pulley system drag me 150 yards up a steep incline while standing on my skis. They told me to keep my skis in the deep ruts in the snow, made by all the previous skiers, or else I could catch my ski and go tumbling down the mountain. That sure got my attention, but at least I could see that others had done this. I hadn't seen the ski patrol rushing up for rescues, so that was a good sign. Now I was shaking like a leaf and holding on for dear life, making sure to keep my skis in the ruts while also trying to keep my poles out of the way so I didn't trip over them. I was a hot mess! And my self-talk wasn't much better: *"Connie, how did you get yourself into this? You're so stupid. There is no way you're skiing down from here. You are never doing this again!"*

CiCi and Patty were waiting for me at the top of the lift. I was so scared that I was sure they could see my heart beating out of my ski jacket like a cartoon character. I told them to go ahead; I was going to find a ski-patrol person to tell me how to get down. But there was only one way down. And now I noticed the sign, the one that shows double black diamonds and says: **"EXPERTS ONLY. Expect unmarked cliffs, rocks, avalanche debris, and other alpine hazards."** Well, I guess the good news was that the sign does not mention random body parts.

We had to take off our skis and climb up a small area of rocky terrain to get to the top of the bowl. The scenery was breathtaking, I could see mountain ranges for miles. We were so high in elevation I felt I could also see the curvature of the earth. I didn't need to look at my trail map to know I didn't belong here. At over 12,000 feet in elevation, trees can't even grow. Clue: If trees can't survive here, I probably can't either. This was a horrible mistake, and I was going to pay the price. I had just had my F#*k Everything And Run moment, but there was nowhere to run. In my ski boots, I walked as close to the edge as I could stand to get and tried to peek over, but I couldn't see anything. It looked like a straight drop. This was it. I was a goner.

Patty, CiCi, and I were now on our skis at the edge of the bowl. I was standing there facing the abyss, me and all my original programming. I had done no personal work up to this point in my life. I knew nothing about fear, or what I now teach about breaking through fear. CiCi gave us a pep talk, waited a few minutes, smiled, and dropped into the bowl. I think on some level she knew that, if she didn't go, we would stand there until darkness fell. Patty waited for me, and I didn't budge, so she dropped into the bowl. Just like that, I was alone, just like any friend you have ever left behind because you knew they just needed to stop talking about something and get on with it already.

I watched others ski up next to me and disappear over the edge without much thought or delay. Obviously, they belonged here. They'd probably been skiing since they could walk. I grew up in Fort Lauderdale, at sea level, where we didn't even have hills for goodness sake. I didn't want to die or suffer serious injury. What if there were big boulders down there? Oh no! I could break my legs and have to be airlifted off the mountain, in traction for months.

I couldn't stay up there all night and risk frostbite. So, with no other way out, I made my deal with God: "Please, God, let me live! I promise I will be *so* good. I will never curse again. Use me in any way you want. Just. Let. Me. Live!" And with that, I pushed myself off the edge of the mountain and freefell into the bowl. As soon as I hit, I realized my legs were gone. They were not actually gone, but they were lost under two feet of soft powder. I actually landed upright on my skis. I couldn't believe it. "I'm alive! I'm alive!" I was now racing straight down the mountain and picking up speed fast. I knew I wouldn't be alive much longer if I didn't start making some cuts and turns to slow myself down. I went from feeling sheer terror to exhilaration in a matter of seconds, once I realized I'd survived.

We've all been in over our head, and it's a tremendous experience when you do get through it. In a lot of these situations, it just takes everything you've got—your whole being—to figure out how to do it. Because most times, as much as you want to F#*k Everything And Run, you can't. It's just not possible. It's not an option.

Fear is a natural emotion when you find yourself in over your head. It doesn't matter how you got there; once there, you need to find your way out. How you react to your fear will determine how you get through any extreme difficulty or serious trouble. It isn't always physical danger you are in either; sometimes it's your ego that's hanging in the balance.

My first time skiing the bowl was with my very limiting, existing fear programming, which left me with only my F.E.A.R. mindset: F#*k Everything And Run. When I could not actually run, quit, or chicken out, I had no other alternatives, but my mindset left me in a very unresourceful state.

My reaction to my fear led me to see only my limitations, and I exacerbated it with my negative thinking and self-talk. Inside my head, it looked something like this: "*I definitely don't belong on this double-black-diamond trail and am stupid for even thinking that I do. I made a horrible mistake, and since mistakes aren't allowed, I'll probably pay a price, in this case, with injury. Everyone up on the bowl is so much better than me; I can't compete with them. I have nowhere near the skills I need to ski down from here. There are probably huge boulders down there, just under a light covering of snow. If I hit one, I'll need to be rescued by ski patrol, and I'll be on the mend for months, not to mention the pain.*"

Geez, with all this going on in my head, it's no wonder that it took me so long to take the leap. Knowing what I know now, I don't think there is much more I could have done to myself to make this a more horrible situation. Fortunately for me now, years of my own experience breaking through fear has allowed me to alter my programming and transform my mindset to F.E.A.R. meaning "False Evidence Appearing Real."

If I were to find myself standing on the edge of that bowl today, I would be more aware and able to quickly identify my feeling of fear, and I would disrupt my pattern with the following conscious thoughts: "*I am feeling fear, and I am okay right now. I've never skied a bowl before, but I see others dropping over the edge, so it must be possible. My skiing has improved by leaps and bounds over the last few days, so maybe I can do this. CiCi is a nurse, and Patty is a police officer; both are public servants and seem to be reasonable people. I don't think they would put me in a life-threatening situation. CiCi must know Patty and I are ready for this challenge, or else she wouldn't have brought us up here. Certainly, the ski patrol would have put up ropes to keep us out of the areas where boulders and rocks are hazardous.*"

"False Evidence Appearing Real" doesn't mean that I pretend that actual danger doesn't exist, but it does give me an opportunity to respond to it instead of reacting or being paralyzed into inaction. Feeling that I didn't belong on a double black diamond was False Evidence Appearing Real. I had been skiing black-diamond trails all day. This was part of my progression in becoming an expert skier. Was I stupid because I ended up on the bowl? Nope. False Evidence Appearing Real. Am I really not allowed to make mistakes? Again, no. This is ridiculous. I am human. False Evidence Appearing Real. Was there a pile of bodies lying on rocks below? Of course not. False Evidence Appearing Real. The ski resort would never put skiers in a position like this without warning.

If you found yourself in over your head in my ski situation, which mindset would you want for yourself? "F#*k Everything And Run" or "False Evidence Appearing Real." The choice is clear, and the choice is yours. I think you'll agree that the scenario experienced with a False Evidence Appearing Real mindset would put you in a more resourceful state, making it much easier to muster the courage to push yourself off that mountain. You might have even been able to embrace your fear and fall into the deep powder with a smile on your face.

It might take a little effort at first, but you can transform your programming to become much more resourceful once you realize you're in over your head. The first step, as always, is to become aware and acknowledge that you are experiencing fear. Slow down your thinking, and assess your situation, eliminating emotion if possible. This will help you choose your response rather than reacting impulsively. When you decide on the action you want to take, clear your mind of all the self-limiting thoughts, fear, and negative self-talk; push all the bad stuff that you think is going to happen out of your head. As you take your action, focus on what you want to happen. Take a chance and decide to be all in. It might be that there's no other way; this is your only choice, and you've got to get yourself to the point where you can take that action.

Questions, although not always an option, are a great tool to help keep ourselves from getting in over our heads. The better the questions, the better the answers. In hindsight, I could have asked CiCi some questions about the level of difficulty I was about to face, and why she thought I was ready for it. I'm going to caution you here though, not to ask too many questions. Asking more questions would have given me a better idea of what to expect once I got to the top, but it also might have kept me from the experience. Don't ask so many questions that you talk yourself out of the thrills life puts in your path.

"In over your head" suggests situations that are dangerous or should be avoided at all cost, but this is not always the case. Some fearful, or "in over your head" situations are not physically dangerous at all. Imagine you are traveling across the country to assist in a presentation to your company's top client. The night before the presentation, you find out the main presenter has been snowed in, and their flight has been canceled. You get word from your boss that you are going to present alone, because like in show business, the show must go on. You have no choice. Luckily, you have attended a few presentations, and you have a pretty good idea of how it's supposed to go. You go through the steps I mentioned above with a False Evidence Appearing Real mindset and give it all you've got, because that's all you can do. You might be surprised to see you actually rise to the occasion.

If you want to improve in a sport, play with someone better than you. Reaching their level of competition might mean getting beat a lot in the beginning as you improve your skills. A beginner skier doesn't become an intermediate skier just by moving from green to blue trails. They're probably going to take a few falls on the blue trails along the way. Skiing with CiCi took me from being an intermediate skier to a solid expert skier in just one week. It was invigorating to push myself to keep up, and find that I could break through my fear every time I found myself on a trail that was beyond my perceived ability. Same goes for work too. If you have the mental and emotional capacity, you will grow considerably from these types of situations. And eventually, you will seek them out instead of avoiding them, welcoming the opportunity to grow.

I didn't realize at the time how skiing the bowl with CiCi would have a hand in changing my relationship with fear. One moment, I thought I was dropping to my death. Within seconds, I found myself in deep powder, upright on my skis. Not at all what I was expecting. Once I found my legs, in an instant, my emotions swung to the opposite end of the spectrum, from fear to exhilaration. I rushed down to meet my friends, to revel in my triumph. Once I skied the top of the mountain the first time, my self-doubt and fear never came back. It is amazing how quickly we can change our idea of what we think we're capable of. We continued to ride the chairlift and T-bar lift up to the top of the mountain and skied the bowl for the rest of the day, something I swore to myself I would *never* do again! All these years later, this is still one of the best days of my life. And the truth is, I *never* would have experienced it if there had been an easier way down.

Now, back to you standing on the third floor of your office building. When the firefighter points at you to climb down first, how do you react? Time is of the essence, and what you do next matters. You go, of course, because this is your only way out. She picked you because she senses you have it in you to do it. It is now your opportunity to lead. Trusting the well-trained firefighters to get you down safely, you follow the instructions to crawl out the window and onto the ladder. Focusing on every wrung of the ladder, you get yourself down quickly. Once on the ground, you feel a huge surge of courage, like you've never felt before, even though you are still shaking from the experience. You don't know it, but your co-workers are inspired by your bravery. You shout encouragement up to your coworkers: "You can do it. Just a little bit more. You're almost there. You got this." Eventually everyone makes it to safety.

This will be a day at work you'll never forget. You will be asked by friends and family to retell this story at gatherings for the rest of your life. You'll relive this experience each time you tell the story, remembering the fear, the concern on your coworkers' faces, the smell of smoke, and the sound of the sirens. And this day will be one of your greatest triumphs, because you broke through in the most unexpected way. This day will change you. This will be one of the greatest days of your life!

" Vulnerability sounds like truth and feels like courage. Truth and courage aren't always comfortable, but they're never weakness. "

— **Brené Brown**
American professor, researcher, author, lecturer

CHAPTER SEVEN

Vulnerability – Your Subtle Superpower

Like fear, vulnerability comes in many forms, centered around possible exposure to physical or emotional harm or attack. Many of our vulnerabilities are felt very deeply, leading us to go to great measures to avoid situations where we might feel vulnerable. Vulnerability around physical harm, depending on our career and lifestyle, is the easiest to manage. Being mindful and making good decisions helps keep us safe from everyday dangers, where we might hurt our physical body. Protecting our emotional body is a lot more complicated. As we seek connection to others in our personal and professional lives, we put ourselves at emotional risk. The greater the connection we need or desire, the more we will be required to open ourselves up, showing more of who we really are. The deeper the self-disclosure, the greater the risk of feeling fears of rejection, judgment, hurt, and failure, along with the uncertainty that comes with it all.

Since you're reading about vulnerability, I'm going to share a secret with you. I have never had the desire to be an author or write a book. So how did I get here? I'm glad you asked. I was strongly encouraged by several people I respect, and who know me well, to write a book. I found myself with time on my hands, and no reason not to, so here I am writing this book. My only stipulation was that it had to be meaningful to you, the reader. It's not worth it for me to go through all this hard work just to say I wrote a book.

The act of writing, and deciding what to include, has left me in a vulnerable state. How much of myself do I put out there to the world, to live forever in print? Will I have enough content valuable to the reader to complete this book, or will I discover a few months from now that I have wasted my time? Is it normal to feel nauseous after every chapter is complete, knowing I have to decide on something else of value to write? Lastly, why write about vulnerability when renowned researcher and author Brené Brown has already shared her work with the world?

Secret number two: My previous question shows how I can sometimes suffer from comparisons to others—my judgment of self. I am including in this book what I have learned about vulnerability in my own life experience, and in my work with others as they face their fears. I'm giving you what I have learned about vulnerability from my perspective.

Anyone with a fear of judgment might read the prior paragraph and cringe at the thought of me being so vulnerable, putting all that out there. Why would anyone openly admit those deep feelings, which could possibly lead others to think they are inadequate, or inferior to someone else? Isn't it embarrassing to admit all that? What if people see you as weak? Up until my mid- twenties, I would have agreed with you.

I was always a highly self-conscious person, and it didn't really subside to a healthy level until I started to face my fears and do my own personal work, which led to self-awareness. Self-awareness enabled me to learn to accept myself and become more aware of my emotions and those of the people around me. With my self-acceptance also came a healthy dose of self-esteem. All of this makes it possible for me to share at a deep level in order to help others.

It's almost impossible to live life without being vulnerable. If you try to avoid facing the fear of judgment, fear of hurt, fear of failure, and fear of rejection, you'll need to live a life of isolation. Most of us prefer not to live like that, so we resign ourselves to a certain level of vulnerability. Limiting our chance of exposure to these vulnerabilities also means limiting opportunities in our personal and professional lives and increasing our stress level as we hide our true selves from others.

If your goals and dreams are important to you, you are going to be required to grow in order to achieve them, or else you would have already attained them. The amount you grow will be determined by how much judgment, rejection, failure, and hurt you are willing to endure. And just like other fears that you have already broken through, the more you open yourself up to these vulnerabilities, the less effect they will have on you.

When I work with people, they often have an opportunity to break a board with their bare hands. To an observer, this might look like a purely physical activity, but it is actually more mental than physical. From the moment they have the board in their hands, their mind is going a mile a minute. I see knuckles knocking on the boards, panicked eyeballs checking out the thickness of the boards, and hear nervous laughter filling the room. I have their full attention as I take them through the process, getting them ready for their breakthrough.

Attendees might think they are just breaking through their self-identified fear or limiting belief, but they are working on so much more than they are aware of. If they are in the presence of people they work with or know well, they will also be working on a deeper emotional level. You see, I don't just ask them to break a board with their bare hands. I ask them to first write one of their fears or self-limiting beliefs on that board, giving them the opportunity to then break through them, both physically and mentally.

Those attendees preparing to do the exercise in front of friends, colleagues, or even strangers also have to decide how real they want to be with what they write on their board. Identifying a fear or limiting belief in your head is one thing; writing it across your board for others to see takes it to another level, leaving them to ponder, *How honest am I willing to be with myself and others?* And when it comes time to break the board, they may think, *What if I can't break my board? What if I don't succeed? If I don't attempt it, how will I be judged? Is it okay for me to fail in front of others? If I get hurt, is it worth it? What if no one wants to help me with my board breaking?*

Men and women both experience vulnerability but often in different ways. I have seen men look totally relieved when their board breaks, even at times hearing one say, out loud, "Thank goodness! I didn't want to be *that* guy!" This always gets a laugh, because the men in the room can relate to that feeling. He doesn't want to be the guy that fails in front of other people. What would that do to the image he is projecting of male strength?

Women break boards just as easily as men, yet occasionally, when a woman breaks a board, she'll look astonished. I'll watch her go from fierce determination to stunned when the board breaks in half. After astonishment comes elation and celebration. Maybe at some point, she thought, *There's no way I'm going to be able to do this.* Once she does, she discovers the power of her mind. It's great for men to see women break through boards or concrete blocks, and for women to see men be vulnerable. As society continues moving towards gender equality, it helps us expand our roles, allowing men and women to both be strong and vulnerable.

One of the reasons vulnerabilities are so uncomfortable is that they are often seen as a form of weakness. This is untrue, of course, and the dichotomy between the perception of being weak, in the beginning of the board-breaking process, and the courage it takes to overcome that perception and break a board with your bare hand is why it is so powerful and transformational. Vulnerability is a superpower that we can use to achieve success!

It takes courage to show your vulnerability, and in my experience, courage is contagious. When the sound of boards breaking and cheering begins to fill the room, people want some of that for themselves. Inspired by what others are accomplishing, they become focused on what they want from the experience, which is their own breakthrough. In that moment, what they want to achieve is greater than the need to avoid feeling vulnerable. With the encouragement and support of others, they tap into their superpower and take action. Whether the board breaks or not, this isn't the determining factor for the level of breakthrough. For some people, the courage to make an attempt will create change.

You might think that not being able to proclaim fearlessness would be a liability for someone who teaches others how to break through fear, but it's not. It's actually an asset—a tool that I use that helps me build rapport with the audience. When I stand in front of a group and get them ready to break boards with their bare hands, or walk barefoot across hot coals, I can sense the fear, self-doubt, and uneasiness. I know they're going to be fine, but they're not so sure. I understand exactly what they're going through, because I've been there, and I'm going to be honest about the physical risk they are taking and decisions they will need to make. I also know the freedom that's waiting for them on the other side of that board or coal bed. My job is to help them to find within themselves whatever it is they need in order to get to the other side, to overcome, so they can experience their own breakthrough, and hopefully apply what they learned to other real-world situations.

I leverage my vulnerability and honesty from the stage so that I can gain trust. I can't expect them to be something I'm not willing to be. I want them to see value in vulnerability. I could never stand in front of people and lead them to believe that I am fearless and tell them that, if they do what I do, they can be fearless just like me. First of all, when people lie or misrepresent who they are, I believe others can see right through it. I am an authentic leader, so I share from my own experience, letting people know I am just like them. And if I can do it, anybody can, and then I show them the way.

I've seen a lot of amazing displays of vulnerability from the front of the room. One of the situations that has stuck with me was the transformation of a woman in a small group event. When she came to the front of the group to break her board, she just couldn't do it. After several attempts, she left the room upset, but she didn't leave the premises. Through a window, I could see her pacing outside. I continued to teach as Karen, my co-facilitator, went outside to talk to her.

About twenty minutes later, she returned to the room. Talk about vulnerability! She perceived that she had failed in front of the group, was convinced she could not succeed, quit, and then returned to face possible judgment. During her discussion with Karen, she realized she actually needed to ask for help. She shared that this was something she would rarely do out in the real world, because she felt she needed to be strong. In her very vulnerable state, she asked several women to come to the front of the room to help her. With them standing around her for support, she broke the board with her foot. The entire room erupted with cheers, clapping, and wild high-fiving as we were all witness to her breakthrough.

The breakthrough this brave woman needed was to change her mindset about what asking for help means: It's a sign of strength, not weakness. It wouldn't have happened if she had easily broken the board with her hand. She continued to have success with all the breakthrough activities for the rest of the evening. When it came time to walk on the fire, she did that too. In her firewalk picture, she is exuding confidence and grace as she crosses the coal bed while looking down at the red glowing embers.

A few years later, Karen received an email from the woman, thanking us for her firewalk experience. Turns out, she had moved to Taiwan, where she'd been teaching for the past two years. She shared, "I brought my firewalk photo, and once in a while when I am feeling uncomfortable about living in such a different country, I remind myself that I am not afraid." Talk about living courageously! The beauty of her story is that her walk back into the room was much more difficult than her barefoot walk across a bed of hot coals. It was where her transformation began. She had discovered her superpower!

This was all her doing; I take no credit for what she achieved. It would never have happened had she not had the courage to face the emotional discomfort of her vulnerabilities. She took a huge risk disclosing so much of herself that evening, and she grew tremendously from the experience. I'd like to think she returned to the room because she felt it was safe to do so; she trusted me.

In a recent interview, I was asked when I had made the deliberate decision to show my vulnerability from the stage, and if I felt it made me a better presenter. Yes, I absolutely believe it makes me a better presenter, especially for the content I am presenting. It actually wasn't a decision at all; it is just the way I've presented from day one. Beginning with facilitating my very first firewalk, I was my natural self, which is honest and genuine. I didn't know of any other way to be. Maybe I would have changed things up if I wasn't getting good results, but in my very first event, all participants completed every challenge successfully, without injury, so I just kept the same formula.

My formula works for me. My vulnerability is a tool I use, because to lead anybody, they need to trust you. In leading people through a process of change, I am often putting them through several breakthrough activities (which can be dangerous) in a short timeframe. My honesty helps people feel more at ease, so they are open to being vulnerable themselves in facing their fears. To create lasting change, I'm asking them to do a lot, so I feel like I have to give a lot, and what I have to give is myself. Trust is the foundation for leadership.

Let me caution you: Vulnerability is not a badge to wear, as a beacon of our virtue. It is a natural way of being, allowing vulnerability to subtly flow through everything we do. Discernment will guide us to know how much of ourselves to share, and with whom. We don't want to come across as heavy handed in our approach. While we may be comfortable opening ourselves up at a deep level, it is important to give others the opportunity and space to grow their level of vulnerability. It is unrealistic to expect them to meet us at our level before they feel comfortable doing so.

Whether you are a leader, aspiring leader, or employee, you are constantly dealing with your own vulnerabilities as you navigate your workplace. A leader does not have less likelihood of being affected by fear of rejection, fear of judgment, fear of hurt, or fear of failure by virtue of their position alone. Hopefully, along with all the other skills acquired in leadership development, a leader has also gained self-awareness and emotional intelligence. They will need these skills to set the tone for the level of vulnerability that is safe and/or expected among their team. A leader's behavior will serve as the model for others to follow. It sets the standard.

If you think your emotional behavior as a leader doesn't affect your team, think again. A few years ago, I was called to help a company address low morale and laziness among their employees. During a team-building event, I was impressed with the level of engagement and dedication from the employees, and how highly they spoke of their jobs and their customers. Outside of the office environment, they seemed to enjoy each other's company and worked well together to complete challenges. All my facilitators and I came to the same conclusion: They were a high-functioning team. The behavior did not match in the slightest bit how one of the top executive leaders described his workforce.

Soon after, I facilitated a training for a division within the same company, where they wanted to incorporate a widely used personal-assessment tool to allow everyone to better understand how their different personalities could work better together to thrive at work. The morning of the training, more than half of the employees showed up without the printouts of their assessments. I was perplexed, as they had been instructed (and also reminded the day before) to bring the printouts. While most employees arrived fifteen minutes early, the leader arrived thirty minutes late. Upon arrival, the leader, who happened to be the same top executive mentioned earlier, called me outside. In a whisper, he asked me not to share anything about his assessment. He didn't want anyone knowing what was on the report, especially the part about manipulation.

Bingo! Within a few seconds, the real issue became crystal clear. This top executive led with manipulation and fostered an environment of mistrust. This is why the employees did not bring their personal assessments. They did not trust their boss with the information. This man's fears of rejection, failure, hurt, and judgment caused him to hide his vulnerability and lack empathy. His desire to hide himself caused him to not be able to see the employees for who they really were. I would come to discover that the employees really loved the work they did within the company, yet felt total lack of trust in leadership and undervalued as people. What the executive leader perceived as a problem of low morale and laziness was his effort to project an air of superiority to hide his own insecurities. One person was able to create company-wide dysfunction.

If you were an employee working within this company, you might find yourself afraid to make mistakes, and if you made a mistake, you might be inclined to try to hide it rather than deal with the wrath or judgment of your boss. Would you feel safe opening up at work, exposing any of your soft spots? Probably not. You can picture a manipulative person using anything you share against you, or possibly using it to take advantage of you. "So, you feel like you need to improve in this area? Great. Here's two months' worth of extra work to help you sharpen your skills." It is important, no matter what level you are, to be discerning when deciding how much you want to open yourself up. You don't need to wear all your vulnerabilities on your sleeve to be a genuine person. Boundaries are a healthy part of every relationship.

This is the worst-case scenario I have ever encountered. I am going to trust that, if you are a leader, you like to grow, and with all growth comes acceptance of the risk and uncertainty of facing rejection, judgment, hurt, and failure. As a leader, you might also have a boss, and it's unrealistic to think your boss is going to agree to every great idea you have. You have to be willing to face your fear of rejection. Maybe your boss does buy into one of your ideas, and it turns out to be a total flop. You can decide to be totally crushed and deflated, vowing to never put yourself out there like that again, or you can learn from your mistakes and search for your next great idea. You'll learn the most from the biggest mistakes you make. It's all part of the growth process.

When a leader models a willingness to be vulnerable, they are giving their team permission to do the same. Would you rather have your team willing to take risks, bringing you every idea they have, or sit on their ideas for fear of being judged or rejected? Of course, you want their ideas! This exchange of ideas and knowledge creates a team environment, rather than one where you sit high on the mountain top, unapproachable and all knowing. A vulnerable leader will not only be approachable but will willingly offer insights from their own personal experience, such as pitfalls to watch out for, mistakes they've made and what they learned from them, and any advice that can help others grow. They'll also admit when they don't have all the answers. Authentic leaders share their story—how they got to where they are and what they learned along the way.

It doesn't take elaborate or grand gestures to create an environment where vulnerability is valued. It can be as simple as consistent random action. I observed this type of action during a breakthrough seminar I was facilitating. The leader of the organization spontaneously came to the front of his group, holding his board high above his head. He shared what he had written on his board and stated that he was afraid he wouldn't be able to break it. He asked for a show of hands of anyone experiencing the same fear. Almost every hand in the room went up. In revealing what he had written and sharing his own fear of failure, he modeled a deep level of vulnerability. Trusting him, they were able to follow his lead without fear of judgment. Authentic leadership in action.

If you were able to choose, who would you rather work for? This man or the executive leader I mentioned earlier? Which leader would bring out the best in you? Which leader would make you feel comfortable being your true self? Which leader would you trust? Which leader would inspire and encourage you to grow? Which leader would you work harder for? I think the choice is clear. Obviously, the second leader has emotional intelligence, is secure, genuine, confident, and self-aware. He took advantage of an opportunity to empower his entire group to grow, individually and together.

Speaking of growth, if you are a person who often feels judged by others, overcoming your fear of judgment will radically change your life. As humans, we are constantly judging and comparing; it's how we make decisions. I recently dined at a fine restaurant. As the host led me to my table, I passed a beautiful display of desserts. Cheesecake, souffle, chocolate lava cake, white chocolate mousse, strawberry sponge cake ... all looking delicious and garnished with chocolate or strawberry drizzle, grated chocolate, or fresh fruit. I stopped for a few seconds, sized them all up, and made my decision. Luckily, desserts don't have feelings, or else I would have had to order one of each so that none felt judged and rejected.

A silly example to be sure. I'm using it to illustrate that, as quickly as I judged the desserts, they shortly left my consciousness, except for the one I ordered as my final course. Yum! The same is often true of situations where you might feel you are being judged. That person will probably not hold onto that judgment forever; it will soon leave their consciousness. People who lack self-aware-ness or need to feel better about themselves might habitually judge others. It's not about making you feel bad; its purpose is to make themselves feel better.

There is no shortage of situations where you have the opportu-nity to be judged, and no shortage of reasons either. You can fear being judged if you're not successful at something. Unfortunately, being successful does not guarantee you won't be judged. If someone is jealous of you, it could instigate even more judgment. Judgment from others is something you have no control over. It's inevitable; although, I bet it actually happens less often than you think. Unless you're an accomplished mind reader, you have no idea what someone is actually thinking when you suspect you are being judged.

We often take things that are impersonal and make them personal. Although it's often easier said than done, don't take anything personally. Author don Miguel Ruiz writes about the freedom that comes from this mindset. Nothing other people do is because of you. It is because of themselves. If someone says to you, "Hey, you are so stupid," that is about them, not you. If you take it personally, perhaps *you* believe you are stupid. We often feel judged in areas where we feel deficient. In chapters fourteen and fifteen, we will learn how to break through these types of beliefs without self-judgment.

Even when a situation seems so personal, even if others insult you directly, it has nothing to do with you. What they say, what they do, and the opinions they give are in accordance with the agree-ments they have in their own minds. Their point of view comes from all the programming they received during their upbringing.[5]

---

5   Ruiz, M.D., Miguel Angel (1997). *The Four Agreements: A Practical Guide to Personal Freedom* (p. 47-49). San Rafael, CA: Amber Allen Publishing, Inc.

You can't control the behavior of others, but you can control your own by deciding not to engage when you feel you're being judged. It is none of your business what other people think of you, just as it is none of their business what is going on in your head. You will grow tremendously in this area as you become more self-aware. Since fear of judgment is an emotion, if you conquer that fear, you will no longer feel the need for validation or acceptance from others. You will be free of your concern about what others think of you. You will be able to enjoy connection with others, knowing that while judgment, hurt, rejection, and failure may come, you don't need to fear it. It takes courage to be yourself, and no one in the world is as good at it as you. Be courageous and use your subtle superpower of vulnerability. The rewards are worth it!

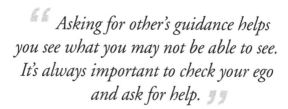

*" Asking for other's guidance helps
you see what you may not be able to see.
It's always important to check your ego
and ask for help. "*

— Ken Blanchard
American author, motivational speaker

CHAPTER EIGHT

FOAFH – It's a Thing

By now you understand the concept of fear as an emotion that will affect what we will accomplish in life. The entire spectrum of emotions is a mainstay of our existence, and how we manage it will determine our success. Notice I used the word "manage" rather than "control." We cannot control whether we feel the emotion of fear, but we can learn to manage our thoughts and actions when in the midst of feeling it. This is the cornerstone for living courageously. People who appear fearless have learned to master their fear, instead of allowing it to master them. With enough practice and conscious action to face fear and break through it, you will create a paradigm shift, empowering you to embrace fear.

Fear is pernicious, and there is no shortage of opportunities to practice breaking through it, especially if you are striving for greater success in your life. Just as it is unrealistic to expect to never feel fear, we must also accept the fact that we have vulnerabilities. There is no escaping this human condition, although many of us will try with all our might. One of the most uncomfortable vulnerabilities we experience is when we require help from others. None of us is above the fear of asking for help. It's a thing. There is even a hashtag for it: #FOAFH!

No matter how accomplished we are, we all need help sometimes. The best lawyer in the world will seek the help of representation if they should find themselves on the wrong side of the law. As they say, "A lawyer who represents himself has a fool for a client." When Tiger Woods was the number-one golfer in the world, he was working with coaches to help him change his swing. Who knows more about winning form than Tiger Woods? Even he sought help while at the top of his game, and he didn't care if the whole world knew it. He kept his eye on the prize.

We don't need to experience the drama of a lawyer fighting to save their own career in the courtroom, or the golfer trying to remain number one, to know the fear that comes with asking for help. We are all familiar with this fear of having to reach out to someone for assistance, and just like all our other fears, we can develop the skills to break through this one.

Putting off facing our fear does not diminish it, or else we would all have mastered the game of waiting for it to pass. The sooner we recognize this and lose the idea that we're above asking for help, the sooner we will be able to face our fear, allowing us to move on from whatever problem we can't solve on our own or challenging situation we find ourself in. Quick recognition of this opportunity to face our FOAFH will speed up our personal and professional development for the betterment of our life and career.

Mentoring or coaching is a great way to develop our talent. Establishing a relationship with someone dedicated to aiding in our growth will definitely help ease the stress and fear that comes with career advancement. A mentor or coach is not there to solve problems for us but rather to help expose us to new behaviors and new ways of thinking that we will then use to solve our own problems. Being able to ask for help and receive feedback and critique is invaluable. Should this type of supportive relationship be available to you, it is a great place to begin conquering the FOAFH.

When I present breakthrough activities, opportunity frequently arises where the audience will be directed to ask one another for help. When this occurs, there is often a pause where people will look around the room, waiting to see if others are really going to do it—actually ask someone else to help them in front of other people. Eventually they do, once they realize I'm not kidding.

Even in this fun environment, I can sense the discomfort. Some people actually find it difficult to say the words, "Will you help me?" I once worked with a man and woman for about three minutes as they struggled to grasp my direction. They kept offering to help each other, instead of asking for help. "Can I help you with that?" he eagerly asked. "Sure, can I help you with that?" she replied with a smile. It was comical and took quite a bit of work to help them realize how hard it was for them to even speak the words. They both shared with the group that asking for help would be the last resort in real-life situations, a "break glass in case of emergency" crisis. It's fitting how they unknowingly paired themselves up so they could mirror each other's FOAFH.

When the need to ask for help is reciprocal, as in the situation just mentioned, it is a little easier for many people. There is comfort in knowing we are not the only one in need of help, and the pleasure of being helpful is beneficial in easing our pain. It's much more difficult when it's a one-way street, because often in the workplace we don't have that offer, or a situation where we can reciprocate, so we have to learn to ask for help. We have different reasons for our FOAFH, depending on the situation. Here are a few of the many reasons people resist asking for help.

Fear of rejection is probably the most common reason we fear asking for help. It takes a lot to get up the courage to put our self out there and admit we need help. If we hear "No," it means we're going to have to gather the courage to do it all over again, which can be overwhelming to consider. Sometimes we take "No" personally, which can negatively affect our self-esteem, or we can get angry and aggressive. Much of our distress around rejection is self-inflicted. It's important to keep things in perspective and realize this happens to everyone. Is it possible we were told "No" because they actually *can't* help us, rather than *won't?* No one likes to hear "No," but I would rather hear "No" than "Maybe" or "I'll try." It's better to receive the refusal to help than the false hope of help that never comes.

Appearing weak is a common reason we avoid asking for help, especially in the workplace. This should go without saying, but asking for help is a sign of strength, not weakness. A strong, secure person who knows what they want and need will be willing to ask for help. A weak or insecure person will hide the fact that they need help, staying stuck in the process. There is great strength in being willing to stand in the face of fear and admit what we don't know or can't do alone.

Pride and ego can stand in the way of asking for help. Prideful people take pleasure in their own achievements, and often that can mean achieving it at the exclusion of other's help or assistance—leading to the mindset that says, "Success should be mine and mine alone." In an effort to protect our ego, our sense of self-importance and self-worth, we feel we should not need the help of others, and if we do, it damages our personal identity. Pride can make us think we should be able to accomplish everything on our own.

Next, some of us can't stand the thought of an **I.O.U.** (I owe you) existing out there. If someone helps us, surely we are going to be expected to reciprocate at a later date, and we worry we might get taken advantage of. This type of person is always keeping score. Keeping the scales balanced is important and owing somebody something can make us feel like we have no control of fairness.

Not wanting to be a bother makes it very difficult to ask for help. Beginning a request for help with "I don't want to bother you, but...." implies that we already think we are inconveniencing, troubling, or disrupting another person, which is not a very convincing way to ask for help. There could be a lot behind this reasoning, but it is very painful to watch someone suffer with feeling like they're not worth other people's time or effort, like they don't want to be a burden, or thinking that other people are more important, that their own opinions don't matter, and that nobody wants to hear what they have to say. These feelings and beliefs might be an indication that they lack self-esteem and self-worth.

There is a fascinating imbalance between asking for help and a willingness to be helpful. I have asked this question to groups of all types and sizes for over fifteen years, and the answers are always the same. If I ask an audience for a show of hands to indicate that they like to ask for help, maybe a few hands go up, and sometimes none. But if I ask who among them likes to help, nearly everyone's hand goes up. This usually gets a surprised reaction from the audience, and I can see lightbulbs going off over their heads. We're all suffering with the same fear, and the antidote is to learn to ask for help, because this simple exercise makes it clear that plenty of people have the human desire to be helpful.

I like to teach others and also grow myself, which makes me really enjoy helping people. I like learning about people's goals and what they want to accomplish. When helping someone with a problem or situation, there is an opportunity for a greater connection where I might discover their learning style, orientation to fear, and their mindset when faced with a challenge. When appropriate, I share any wisdom I've picked up along the way that I think they might find useful. Oftentimes it is easier to see solutions when I'm not the one so closely affected by the problem or situation.

Most people feel good about helping or doing good deeds for others; it makes us feel useful and needed. Have you ever met anyone who is always running around trying to help or fix people? There is something called a "helper's high," where it literally feels good to help others. Endorphins that are released when we are in the helping mode improve our mood and can even give our self-esteem a boost. Some people can get addicted to this, leading to burnout.

Over the years, I have learned people often experience great struggle just prior to a breakthrough. It's easy to fall into the trap of wanting to help somebody to ease our own discomfort, which is action taken for our own benefit, not theirs. When I reflect on my own life and career, the biggest lessons I learned were after a little struggle or focused attempt to solve a problem. There is a fine line between letting someone figure things out on their own for the sake of learning and coming to the rescue to solve the problem for them. People who are too invested in solving problems for others can go from do-gooders to enablers without even realizing it. This can create an environment where people don't feel empowered to solve their own problems or have the confidence to creatively search for solutions.

If you want people to feel empowered to solve problems and develop creative thinking, they will need an environment where they are not afraid to fail. Of course, professionally, you don't want people making mistakes and wasting company resources just for the sake of feeling good at work. You want to empower them to take calculated risks to find better ways of doing things, for example, searching for ways to increase production and profitability or improve a product or service. If you want to speed up the process and cut down on mistakes or failure along the way, you'll also want to cultivate an environment where people are encouraged to ask each other for help. When there is an opportunity to learn what works and what doesn't work from others, there is less chance of duplicating the same mistakes.

A skilled leader will set the stage for this by conveying the message that, individually (the leader included), not one person alone knows everything, but that collectively, they can share knowledge to contribute to a bigger cause. People need to feel it's safe to admit a lack of skill or knowledge and seek the help of others. A leader can help create this attitude by modeling the behavior, admitting when they don't know something, asking for help when needed, and willingly helping people when asked. A leader will also be aware of letting people grow through the process, letting them struggle for a bit, and if all goes as planned, welcome them asking for help when the time is right.

One trait virtually all leaders share is self-reliance. Self-reliance is viewed as a very positive asset for business leaders, but it can work against you, because it can breed a "loner" mindset, and a hesitancy to ask, or trust, others to help. I learned this the hard way when I owned a printing business with my family in my mid-twenties. I was a workaholic also struggling with fear of success and fear of failure; perfectionism; self-limiting beliefs that I was not good enough; not smart; a desire to make everyone happy; and other dynamics that come with working with family. This all led to a perfect toxic storm inside my head. While I was certainly aware that working sixty to eighty hours a week was not healthy, everything else I was dealing with remained out of my awareness until years later, when I began delving into what makes me tick.

To hide my emotional pain, I learned to mask it. Maybe you can relate to feeling the need to mask certain flaws or deficiencies you think will hold you back or be frowned upon in the workplace. This is very common in the corporate world; we decide what we want to project and wear that mask. Those of us that are good at it take pride in how we're able to fool others. For me, I was great at it, until it almost cost me my life.

I was so good at masking my pain that no family members, friends, or employees knew of my suffering and how close I was to ending my life. My own siblings learned about this for the first time when they read this book. My workaholism and my refusal to ask for help meant I needlessly carried the load. At my breaking point, when I knew there was a good chance I was not going to survive, I went to a psychologist for help. Was it scary to seek help in this way, to share my darkest thoughts with a stranger? Absolutely! This is the greatest example in my life of a time when I desperately needed help. I asked for help, accepted it, and it was the catalyst for all the good in my life today.

I was a year into facilitating firewalks before I realized that what I had planned to use to end my life (fire) was now what I used to help others move forward in theirs. Our life's journey takes interesting twists and turns, and sometimes we need the help of others to weather the storms. I will be forever grateful to my psychologist for helping me save my life.

Times have changed. We now have inspiration from people like Michael Phelps, the most decorated Olympic swimmer of all time, working to destigmatize depression and mental illness. He shared his own lowest point, after the 2012 London Olympics, when he spent a few days in his room, not wanting to be alive. Eventually, he realized there was something he could do. He asked for help and worked with a therapist to save his life. Most of us are not competing on an Olympic level, but there are stressors and challenges that come from striving to reach our goals and be our best. Even with great success there can be trouble coping. Michael Phelps reminds us that we are human—and we are not alone. He is living proof that the best and strongest in the world need to ask for help coping from time to time.

I have decided to include this painful period of my life in hopes that you can learn from my mistakes. If I had had the skills and courage to ask for help in running my business, I would never have reached that low point. Take it from me, asking for help does not need to be your last resort. Asking for help is a tool to help you accomplish and succeed; it's not a sign of weakness, and there's nothing to be embarrassed about.

I'm not going to lie to you and say I enjoy or look forward to asking for help, but it has gotten much easier for me over the years as I learned more about myself. The reason behind your FOAFH doesn't matter. Whether you think it is fear of rejection, not wanting others to think you're weak, not wanting to be a bother, your pride, or any other reason, your result will be the same if you don't take action to break through your fear. You'll be stuck with whatever problem you can't solve on your own or in a bad situation you can't get yourself out of.

None of us is expected to know everything, and it's unrealistic to put that kind of pressure on yourself. There is a learning curve when you are put into a new position or learning new skills, so all you can do is focus on learning, knowing that when you get to a roadblock, it's not a deal breaker. It doesn't mean you are in over your head or that you don't belong in the position. It just means you have hit a point when asking for help is required to progress in your learning. If you want to speed up your learning, you can lessen the time that you struggle and seek help sooner.

Like breaking through any fears, asking for help can be extremely uncomfortable in the beginning, and it will get easier the more you do it. You can change your mindset around asking for help by realizing that sometimes it is part of the learning process, or simply getting things done. Stay focused on what you want to accomplish and eventually you will have a breakthrough and become proficient in your new skill.

As a leader, it's your role to create a supportive environment where people feel safe to take calculated risks, knowing they will occasionally fall short. This is how they learn and innovate.

A small amount of struggle at work is not always a negative and can often lead to a breakthrough in learning or improvement in processes. When struggle is taking place, it is vital to observe the individual and see if they are working their way to a solution or if they are under so much pressure that they are ready to give up in frustration. You don't want to put yourself in a position where you are going around fixing everything for everybody, but you can encourage people to recognize the need to ask for help sooner. Some people will require more encouragement than others to break through their fear of asking for help.

It is wise for leaders to resist the urge to wear the mask of "knowing everything." First, it's not sustainable. Second, nobody willingly or enthusiastically follows a "know it all," but they will move mountains for a humble, respected leader. Occasionally, asking for help from those you lead is a great way to display vulnerability, showing that you are human too. Not only are you communicating through action that asking for help is okay and acceptable but it is also a great way to build up the confidence of those you lead. People do what they see, so what better example than to see it from you, the boss.

FOAFH is a thing, but it doesn't have to be *the* thing that holds you back. To break through your fear of asking for help, start by becoming aware of when you need help. What thoughts or feelings do you have around *the ask?* What is causing the resistance? Remember, the reason for the fear is less important than what you want or need to accomplish.

Embrace vulnerability and start transforming your mindset about what asking for help really is. It is a sign of strength. Strong confident people know they are deserving of help and will be discerning in seeking out the best source for it. Know that, as you set your intention and consciously take action to build this skill of asking for help, you are empowering yourself. Be courageous and keep your eye on the prize.

" *Failure seldom stops you. What stops you is the fear of failure.* "

— Jack Lemmon
American actor

CHAPTER NINE

Fear of Failure

We all fail—a lot. Sometimes our failures are funny. Like the time, as a teenager, when I was playing third base in a softball tournament. After catching a grounder, in one smooth move, I was moving towards first base as I was transitioning into the throwing position. Somehow I ended up getting my cleat stuck in the shoelace of my other shoe. While the bottom of my body was frozen in a twisted mess, the top continued with the throwing motion. I wound up face planting in the orange clay, body fully extended flat in the dirt with my arm straight above my head, pointing towards first base. My hand was still clutching the softball. I was smooth all right. Stunned, I stood up, and the game had stopped. My teammates were hysterical. The other team was laughing. The umpires and fans were laughing too. We laughed until we cried. Officially, this was considered an error, E5 in the scorebook. But this wasn't just your run of the mill, ball between your legs error; this was a dramatic funny failure.

If our failures could consistently bring joy and fun to others, we would have far fewer hang-ups about them. But the truth is that failure is usually not funny or fun. It's painful, and it begins early in life. Remember back in elementary school when your teacher handed back your graded assignment, and you were hoping to see a happy face or big star at the top, only to find red X's, circles, and corrections all over the page? What about the big red minus number at the top, screaming the total number you got wrong? Did you then take your paper home and hear all about how you should have done better? Many of us are still scarred by the red markings, their negative connotations, and our parent's reactions.

We learn and grow through this process of making an effort and then having our performance graded by others. Many of us grow up striving to be right, to be good, and in some cases, to be perfect. When we succeed, our confidence and self-esteem get a huge boost, and we get positive affirmation from others. When we fall short, it can sometimes feel like a punch in the gut, our emotions getting the best of us. Failure can engage many painful emotions like shame, embarrassment, frustration, anger, regret, disappointment, anxiety, and sadness. It's no wonder that an estimated 31 percent of adults are afraid of failure.[6] It makes sense that we learn to avoid feeling the emotional toll that failure brings.

As we develop into adults, we experience two sources for our fear of failure: internal and external. The internal source—by far the greater—is driven by our fear of failing ourselves and all the negative emotions that come with failure. It is true that, for most of us, even when our failures affect others, no one will feel worse about our failure than we do. Nobody can make us feel worse than we already do when we fail, because we have become very proficient in absorbing all the negativity that comes with failure. Sometimes we beat ourselves up for buying into our own wishful

---

6   YouGov PLC, an international research data and analysis group (2015). Fear Factor Index. One in three American adults were found to be afraid of failure (31 percent), 1 percent more than spiders (30 percent).

thinking, believing we could accomplish something that obviously we couldn't. Feeling defeated, we give up. Left unchecked, this emotional turmoil could lead to debilitating pessimism and lack of confidence.

The external source for our fear of failure is similar to our early schooling, except now our performance is being evaluated by our boss or other authority figure. Whereas, with our internal source, we fear disappointing our self, with the external, we fear disappointing others. Failure, in this instance, presents the opportunity for those painful emotions from childhood to arise, like shame, embarrassment, frustration, anger, regret, disappointment, anxiety, and sadness, and adds fault and blame into the mix.

Failure and responsibility often go hand in hand at work, which can make it more emotionally charged. In an effort to improve processes, safety, and profitability, companies will often do a post-mortem to analyze the source, or reason, for the failure. The need for a source can also lead to someone being held responsible. Done right, this is not to assign fault, blame, or to criticize—though it can sure feel like it—but rather to learn from the failure, which can lead to innovation. Done wrong, it can lead to actually blaming someone for the failure, or worse. You could have someone unable to admit failure, who projects it onto someone else, literally blaming someone else for their failure. You can imagine the negative effect all this could have on someone inexperienced in managing their emotions.

Failure at work is not always a bad thing, as it is necessary for innovation. One of our country's greatest inventors, Thomas Edison, is also one of our most famous failures. The number of Edison's failures in creating a carbon filament for the lightbulb is legendary. Depending on the source, the number of attempts he made range between one thousand and ten thousand, although no one knows for sure. I was lucky enough to be friends with Edison's great-grandniece, Sarah Miller Caldicott, who wrote the book *Innovate Like Edison*. Sarah had access to Edison's notebooks and drawings, and even she could not find an accounting. She did find record of another success: the Edison Storage Battery. According to a quote found from one of his laboratory employees, there were close to fifty thousand experiments to develop the storage battery. This makes the creation of the carbon filament look like a breeze!

Thomas Edison enjoyed tremendous success, but he also experienced some pretty enormous and costly failures throughout his life. What gave him determination and perseverance in the face of so much failure? He had an unusual view of failure, facilitated by his happy disposition. Dr. E. G. Acheson, a chemist once employed on Edison's staff, summed it up this way:

"I once made an experiment in Edison's laboratory at Menlo Park during the latter part of 1880, and the results were not as looked for. I considered the experiment a failure, and while bemoaning the results of this apparent failure Mr. Edison entered, and, after learning the facts of the case, cheerfully remarked that I should not look upon it as failure, for he considered every experiment a success, as in all cases it cleared up the atmosphere, even though it failed to accomplish the results sought for, it should prove a valuable lesson for guidance in future work. I believe that Mr. Edison's success as an experimenter was, to a large extent, due to this happy view of all experiments."[7]

---

7   Gelb, Michael J. and Caldicott, Sarah Miller (2007). *Innovate Like Edison – The Success System of America's Greatest Inventor* (p. 53). New York, New York: Dutton

Edison's "happy view of all experiments" helped him persist in the face of adversity, refusing to call an "unexpected outcome" a failure. He believed that most people gave up too soon, walking away from success and accepting failure instead. He said, "Our greatest weakness lies in giving up. The most certain way to succeed is to try just one more time."[8]

We don't have to be inventors to learn from Edison's mindset on failure. While the goal of having a *"happy view of all our failures"* might be a stretch for us mere mortals, we can certainly improve the way we view our attempts and "unexpected outcomes." If we are paying attention, with every "unexpected outcome," we learn what didn't work. We make adjustments, letting each previous attempt guide us in a new direction. Rinse and repeat until we achieve success.

Fear of failure can be so strong that it keeps us from even getting to an actual failure, or as Edison called it, an unexpected outcome. We all have situations in life where we think, "I wish I could just go back to that time, with what I know now; it would be so different!" What would become one of my greatest regrets came my senior year in high school. The following year, all major colleges and universities were transitioning from slow-pitch to fast-pitch softball. I had never seen fast pitch before, and now with my future in sight, it was like the rug was pulled out from under me.

My fear that I would not be able to hit a fast pitch kept me from even wanting to attempt it. I played it safe and accepted a scholarship to a local community college, where slow-pitch softball was still available. Girls I knew and had played against, who were in the same boat as me, went on to accept the larger scholarships, figuring out how to play the new game once they got there. My fear

---

8   Gelb, Michael J. and Caldicott, Sarah Miller (2007). *Innovate Like Edison – The Success System of America's Greatest Inventor* (p. 53). New York, New York: Dutton

of failing was too great. So great, in fact, that I didn't even attempt to learn how to hit a fast pitch. As I look back now, there was no way I couldn't have made the adjustment. There was absolutely no reason why I could not have excelled, except for my own mindset, which is the most vital part in learning anything.

I'm not proud of this, but along with other painful experiences in my life, it informs who I am today. While I did not possess a healthy mindset in regard to fear of failure in my teens, I am now able to use all I learned to help young people overcome their fears. In my case, Thomas Edison was absolutely right. I failed not because I actually failed to achieve something but because I gave up too soon, before I even got started, and *accepted failure.* With my former mindset, I don't think I would have lasted long in Edison's laboratory.

My work is a laboratory of sorts, filled with people experimenting with themselves, finding ways to break through their unproductive and unfulfilling programming, becoming aware of limiting patterns and belief structures, and taking action to disrupt the programming, creating a new and improved mindset in the process. As I watch them work, I can sometimes sense steam pouring out of ears, or lightbulbs going off overhead.

Most people have never experienced the breakthrough activities that I use to help them transform their mindset, so it often presents an opportunity for fear of failure to appear. We often feel this emotion when we are attempting something for the first time, especially in front of others. Because no two humans in my laboratory are identical, I have observed many different behaviors and beliefs around fear of failure and what one does when they achieve an unexpected outcome. The one I'm about to describe I have seen quite a bit, and it might even look familiar to you.

Many years ago, at a local community-empowerment firewalk seminar, there was a woman in her fifties who could not break her board with her bare hand. It was the very first breakthrough activity of the seminar, and she just couldn't do it. She was unable to change her mindset to have success with board breaking. She sat down, looking disappointed, confused, and discouraged, but she didn't give up on herself. Later, when it was her turn, she bent a long piece of steel rebar using the soft part of her throat. She broke an arrow using the same part of her throat. Then she walked barefoot across fifty pounds of broken glass. From the front of the room, I watched this woman literally transform herself with each challenge accepted. Her night ended with a barefoot walk across a fifteen-foot-long bed of glowing red-hot coals! Attempting any one of these things would be amazing, whether you succeeded or not. Just to have the courage to try one of these unusual fear-busting activities would make you a rare breed.

She didn't just attempt, she succeeded! As anyone who has broken an arrow or bent steel rebar with their throat knows, this doesn't happen by accident. It takes a tremendous amount of focus and determination to put an object like that against your throat and step into it with enough force to bend or break it. To walk barefooted across broken glass, and hot coals between 900 – 1,200 degrees? That goes without saying. It takes a tremendous amount of courage and faith. The world now had one more firewalker! When we said goodbye for the evening, she was radiating.

Because this woman was an acquaintance, I ran into her from time to time over the following several months. Every time she saw me, she would talk about how great her experience was at the firewalk, but she never forgot to mention that she didn't break her board. I would remind her, "You walked on fire! You did it all! You're amazing!" She wasn't buying it. I asked her what she wanted to do about it, and she said she wanted to break it. I invited her to my house, and after a little bit of struggle, she did successfully break her board with her bare hand. What a relief—for her and for me!

Three years later, this same woman attended another empowerment firewalk seminar. A few days later, I received a thank-you email, which included, "I felt so much joy when I broke through that board the *first* time." (The emphasis on "first" was hers, not mine.) Twice, she spent an evening accomplishing amazing feats of mental strength and courage, and what stuck with her was the *one* thing she couldn't do on the first try, three years earlier.

No one likes to fail. Believe me; I have asked enough groups and rarely see a hand go up. I get the opposite response when I ask who likes to learn. Although we don't like to fail, and we don't set out to fail, we can learn a tremendous amount when it happens, if we're willing to be open to the lessons.

There is so much great stuff to learn from my fast-pitch softball story and this firewalker's experience. I failed because my fear kept me from even trying. I was very young and had not yet achieved emotional maturity/intelligence, or the awareness of how I let my fears hold me back. I can't go back and change my past; I can only learn from it. I have chosen to use what I learned to help others, so they don't have to make the same mistakes.

If I could go back to my senior year with the mindset I have now, I would have asked someone to help me learn how to hit a fast-pitch softball. That seems like such an obvious solution, but remember, as a shy child filled with fear, this would have been out of my realm of possibility. I would apply to universities and accept a scholarship if offered. I would have trusted the fact that I was able to excel at slow pitch and that I possessed the skills to succeed in fast pitch. I would have given softball and schooling my greatest effort, enjoying the opportunity, learning all I could, and growing from the hardships. And if, for whatever reason, I failed, I would return home to my local community college. Since that is where I ended up anyway, I had absolutely nothing to lose! I'm sure you've heard the saying "failure is not an option." Actually, it is. Failure is the only option when you let your fear stop you from even trying.

That firewalker faced her fears and achieved great success, twice! She accomplished things most will never have the opportunity to do or the courage to attempt. I am inspired by people like her, who show up for an event, willing to do whatever is required to overcome. Yes, slamming her hand into a board that didn't break was obviously an unexpected outcome, but she didn't let it break her. When she sat down after her perceived "failed attempt," I'm pretty sure she wasn't experiencing Edison's "happy view of all experiments." Something did happen though, and I see this often. An unexpected outcome forces us to think and respond in a different way—a way we would never have come to if we'd had immediate success. This is why it is so important to resist deeming an unexpected outcome a failure. For that firewalker, whatever happened in her head between the time she sat down and the time she got up to do her next breakthrough activity transformed her mindset and led her to success.

In an empowerment seminar, when a person has time and space to sit with a "perceived failure," all kinds of things can happen. Many will begin to identify a pattern that has led to the same results in the past. Maybe beginning to recognize a pattern, they get so disgusted, angry, or sad about the result, and what it has cost them in the past, that they are determined not to let it happen again, fueling the fire for future success. I'll never know exactly what goes on inside someone's head without asking, but I have witnessed what happened with that firewalker happen time and time again. Rarely does a person quit on themselves after not breaking their board. Most often, they go on to accomplish every other challenge.

For this type of person, the board-breaking "failure" was not a failure at all but rather the first step in their process of change. To change our mindset, we have to have a reason to change it, by becoming aware of what's working for us and what's not. The unexpected outcome presents an opportunity to disrupt, or break, the pattern and find another way, using what we learned to guide us to the next best action. Failure is not the opposite of success; it's part of the journey … as long as we are willing to keep pushing forward.

That firewalker did have the ability to break through her fears and learn lessons from unexpected outcomes. I'm not sure she was able to let go of the thought of her "failure" though. The fact that she kept bringing up her failed board breaking attempt led me to believe that she held on to perceived failures and possibly minimized success. Some people will focus on their failures and fears as a way to keep them from happening again, but this is counterintuitive. What we focus on expands in our consciousness, causing us to seek out these experiences, or attract them to us. There is no benefit to hold onto failures; actually, dragging around all that baggage in one area of life can spill over to affect us on a larger scale. Have the experience, learn the lesson, and then let it go like Edison did, as if clearing the atmosphere, leaving room for new possibilities.

In business, failure is not an option, it's inevitable, and fear of failure will not help you elude it. Highly successful people have broken through their fear of failure by realizing it is part of the process, instead of seeing it as a signal of the end. They have managed to change their mindset about failure, transforming it from a dampener into an igniter, and you can too.

Changing your mindset to break through your fear of failure will require you to be conscious of your thoughts and responses to failure. This could be a bit painful in the beginning, but it is vital, because to break the pattern, you have to know what the pattern is. Let's begin with the word "failure." In my life, I use the words "failure" and "unexpected outcome" interchangeably. If the word "failure" gives you an emotional charge, you'll want to use "unexpected outcome" until your mindset around failure has shifted. Once you begin to understand failure for what it truly means, you won't have so much negative emotion attached to it, and you won't need to fear it either.

Being able to view failure as an observer, rather than a victim, will be useful in understanding the benefits of failure. Failure happens to all of us, because we're human. It doesn't happen more to you because you're a bad person or you're more deserving of it than others. Yes, we have all experienced failure in our lives, and we have also all experienced success, so it is important to be able to acknowledge failures and resist the urge to consider yourself a failure, because it's just not true. Failing does not make you a failure. Failure is an event, not a personality defect. A pity party is certainly not going to put you in the resourceful state required to learn from failure.

Failure is not personal, so don't make it so. The encoding of failure stays when we make it personal, validating our existing failure programming, and worse. Taking failure personally can perpetuate the sense of "I'm not good enough" and/or "I'm a failure." You can see how all this could impede our ability to learn, negating the actual benefit of failure.

Failure keeps you humble and shows you where you have work to do. People who have courageously overcome great failure in life are less likely to be cocky or arrogant. A humble leader will be aware of the vulnerabilities of others experiencing failure and be more likely to share what they have learned, picking others up instead of putting them down. Consider how different the environment in Thomas Edison's laboratory would have been, if instead of cheerfully reframing Dr. Acheson's unexpected outcome, he made him wrong and treated him as a failure as a person. The leader sets the example for how their people deal with adversity.

Some people fear failure because they are actually seeking to avoid risk or risky situations. Everything in business is achieved by taking some form of risk. If you want your business to grow, you're going to have to take risks, which means you might experience some failure along the way. This is actually useful, because in business, you learn as much from things that don't work as things that do. Do you and your people have the ability to analyze and evaluate what doesn't work and let that information guide what you do next? The growth of your organization will be determined by how much risk you have the courage to take, and how well you respond and adjust to failure.

If you are willing to face failure, you will be able to take more risks, which means you will experience and accomplish more in life. Breaking through your fear of failure can open up a whole new world for you. Where once you avoided or resisted new things because of your fear of failure, you will embrace opportunity. Failure makes you stronger, just like building a muscle. You take an action (lifting a weight), and you get a result (muscle growth and sometimes pain). Sometimes you don't get the result you want, and you can become disappointed, angry, embarrassed, etc. This can sometimes lead you to want to quit, but if your goal is important, this is not an option.

F.A.I.L. stands for "First Attempt In Learning." Sometimes when you are learning a new skill, or taking on a new challenge, you have an unrealistic expectation of getting it right the first time, every time. That's not actually learning, that's doing. Learning is a process that involves much more than thinking. When you learn something by trial and error, you are involving your thought process, emotions, beliefs, intuitive thinking, and senses, just to name a few. Sometimes learning to do something connects new neurons and forms new neural pathways in the brain, so you are literally changing your brain.[9] That's pretty amazing! So, even if you had Einstein's brain, it would be acceptable to have a stumble or two along the way to mastering a new skill.

As a recovering perfectionist, I can attest to how hard it was to get anything started, because the end result would never be good enough—read that as failure. For me, this created a vicious cycle of procrastination, perfectionism, and failure. To break through my fear of failure, I had to commit to taking action, no matter the end result, and if it was a failure, at least I got there sooner; hence I reduced and eventually eliminated my behavior of procrastination. Instead of being perfect, I focused on progress, doing my best, and seeing my best as good enough. There was a lot involved in this, but it truly was life changing. Years later, I would learn of "Fail Forward Fast," which has some similar aspects to the process I went through.

In 2007, Cam Cameron, the new head coach of the Miami Dolphins football team announced his Fail Forward Fast Philosophy. During the preseason, he wanted his players to fail a

---

9 Ackerman, M.Sc., Courtney E. (2020). *What is Neuroplasticity? A Psychologist Explains.* PositivePsychology.com

lot in an effort to get better with each failure. He wanted to create an atmosphere of learning at a faster pace and finding solutions for all of their weak areas to excel forward toward success. The sooner you fail, the sooner you can move on to success. I totally understood the concept, and it made perfect sense to me. From the booing of the fans attending his press conference, I could tell that promoting failure in sport is a hard sell.

In theory, this was a great concept. In execution by the Dolphins, not so much. They would go on to a 1-15 record—that's one win and fifteen losses! They did not lose because of the Fail Forward Fast Philosophy but because of the coach's conservative play calling. He played it safe, unwilling to take the risks necessary to put his team in a position to win. It's hard to win when you're focused on not losing, just as it's hard to succeed when your focused on not failing.

Failure, and how you deal with it, is a key to success. Although this chapter is about how to break through the fear of failure, it is paramount to stay focused on the success. Visualize the successful outcomes you desire and celebrate them when they occur. Create a success journal, to remind yourself of all the gains your risk-taking is producing and all the new things you have learned. Be willing to learn from failures and mistakes, large and small, and resolve to then let them go. In the words of Edison, "Our greatest weakness lies in giving up. The most certain way to succeed is to try just one more time." You no longer have to fear failure. Like Edison, if you are willing to embrace unexpected outcomes, you can look forward to much-anticipated success ahead.

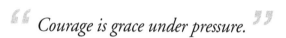

Courage is grace under pressure.

— Ernest Hemingway
American novelist

CHAPTER TEN

Grace Under Pressure

Whether the source of our fear is internal or external, there is no avoiding it, especially if we want to do more and be more in life. Our success depends on our ability to reframe failure from a dead end into something that can guide us—something we can use. Not all failure is created equal, which makes us feel vulnerable in the uncertainty, as we figure out how to make the best of each particular situation.

Some of our failures are funny and will stay with us forever, a source of entertainment for our friends and family. The Internet is filled with people making a living out of capturing other people failing on video. Other failures will come and go, without much effect or fanfare. We'll chalk these up as past mistakes we've made. Failure involving money and other people can be a great learning experience and possibly something that affects the rest of our life, depending on the amount and extent of our entanglement. In life, there are so many opportunities to succeed and fail, so many variables, that it can be overwhelming to consider, and impossible to plan for them all.

Obviously, some failures are bigger than others. A fall on a soft-ball field, if it didn't cost your team the game, can get a big laugh. It will sting a little more and stay with you a little longer if it is the reason for the loss, but life goes on. A trip and fall while walking on a bed of red-hot coals is a much bigger deal and nothing to laugh at. Although I have never seen this happen, it is probably the question I get asked most often, right before we head out to firewalk, showing me that the participants are trying to plan for every eventuality, which is wise in this instance.

In business, a tremendous amount of time and energy goes into strategic planning, and even with flawless execution, success is not guaranteed. A business will experience lots of successes and fail-ures throughout its existence, but it's the big failures that will define it. Failure in business can be costly; often the greater the failure, the greater the financial loss. And it's more than just money on the line; there's reputations and livelihoods to consider too. When all goes as planned, there can be great reward and recognition, with everyone feeling emboldened by success. It's the times when plans fail that a business or organization is really tested.

Challenging times are eventually going to come, and we need to be emotionally prepared to be able to get to the other side. We can't ignore risk, or pretend failure or hardship is never going to happen. In these times, we will benefit from a strong emotional foundation and an understanding of failure and our relationship with it, enabling us to handle the ups and downs as we strive to achieve greater success. Sometimes, when we sense we are heading towards an "unexpected outcome," we have a lot of time to adjust, and other times, we will need to be expeditious in our actions. Often in business, as in life, we need persistence to push through, because quitting in the moment is just not an option.

Don't get me wrong, there are times when quitting, or deciding to scrap a plan and start over from scratch, would be perfectly justified. There is no sense in continuing down the wrong path once you realize you are not going to get the results you want. Create a new and improved plan, implementing what you learned, and begin again. I recently found myself in a situation where this wasn't an option. I had to push through because people were counting on me, more than eight hundred of them, from all over the world. I was hired to speak and facilitate board breaking at a leadership summit. The company was using my presentation to close out their three-day event, where they would hear the CEO's message one last time through me, ending with the leaders breaking boards with their bare hands. Very exciting!

The theme of the meeting was all about bravery, and the CEO had a very clear message. He wanted to encourage his team to take risks, challenge the status quo, be vulnerable, acknowledge successes and failures, and help lift others up through their leadership—all the things brave leadership embodies. I could tell the company was creating a well-planned event, and I would do my part to make sure my team and I were ready. For me, the planning of my work and mental preparation go hand in hand. The more details the better, so that I can focus on what we all need to do to achieve success.

I knew everything that needed to happen, right down to planning for high altitude. Having spent most of my life living at sea level, I was aware this might be a problem, so I flew into Colorado two days early, allowing me to acclimate in the Denver area before heading up into the mountains. Two days of relaxing and drinking enough water to fill a small swimming pool would put me in good condition.

I took in the scenic drive to the mountain ski resort, where I met the client and took care of all the final preparations. I wasn't feeling great, a little short of breath and a headache that wouldn't stop, but I thought I'd be fine in the morning. By the time I ate dinner, I had no appetite and just kept focusing on what needed to happen to make the next morning a success. I was beginning to wonder if I should have given myself more days to acclimate.

The day arrived! I was scheduled to be on stage at 10:55 a.m. for a sixty-five-minute program. I was feeling as bad as I had felt over the previous few days with altitude sickness. It got worse by the hour, but there was nothing I could do about it at that point. At the venue, I was receiving messages from the client with changes to the agenda. No break before I was to take the stage. That's not a problem for me. Then their leaders went over the allotted time with their presentations, so I needed to cut ten minutes to still end on schedule. Then five more minutes was cut from my program. This was not as planned, but there was absolutely nothing I could do about it. Mentally and emotionally, I adjusted to each requested change.

I was wired up and seated amongst the audience, waiting for my time to take the stage. Young leaders were sharing their inspirational stories, which helped take my mind off my altitude sickness. If you have ever experienced altitude sickness or sea sickness, you know the misery I am talking about. You just can't shake it, no matter how hard you try. You are left with no alternative but dealing with it and making the best of it until you have relief. I was looking forward to the energetic music they were scheduled to play as I made my way to the stage, figuring that would help me a bit.

Unfortunately, the speaker right before me was a young male leader who shared about his father and the sadness of his dad's recent death. It was a touching story of overcoming grief and finding a reason to go on. He obviously was picked to illustrate vulnerability in leadership, and the tears of the people seated around me clearly showed he had hit the mark. Because of the subject matter, the event producer informed me that it would be inappropriate to play music as he walked off the stage and I walked on. Of course, that made total sense, but I really needed that music to help get my sick-feeling body up onto that stage.

It was my turn to take the stage. I knew what I needed to do, and I had fifteen minutes less to execute it. I began with a joke, telling them how happy I was to return to the ski resort where I used to ski and how great it was to get reacquainted with my old friend altitude sickness. This drew a lot of laughter. Being in the ski business, they were accustomed to what happens to some people at altitude. I continued my presentation, being aware of my shortness of breath and the pounding in my head that no number of aspirin would alleviate. My team would tell me later that I looked perfectly normal, but on the inside, I felt anything but.

At midpoint, the audience members had their boards in their laps, and they were anxiously awaiting my demonstration so they could pair up and create their breakthroughs. I had my team member Delia come to the stage to hold the board for my board break. I went through my demo, like I have hundreds of times, struck the board, and "smack." It didn't break. Everyone had a good laugh. I made an adjustment in my head, and "smack." Again, it didn't break! Then I realized lack of oxygen from altitude sickness had really taken a toll on my brain and body. I gave it one more attempt, and my board did not break. *Holy, holy, holy crap!*

All of this was happening with more than eight hundred leaders observing, and I'm sure saying to themselves, *"If she can't break it, how can we?"* I needed to be quick on my feet with each failed attempt. After my third attempt, I turned to Delia and said, "It looks like it's going to be you today." The audience laughed, and she looked stunned. Delia had never been on stage before, much less to break a board in front of 1,600 eyeballs, which were now the size of golf balls as they waited to see what happened next. But there Delia was, on stage, probably wondering what she had gotten herself into.

My body felt like I had just run a marathon as I held the board for Delia's attempt. She aimed right at the center of the board, instead of through it, and it didn't break. I was beginning to think this board must be titanium, not wood. I told Delia, "Give it all you got," which drew a laugh from the audience. I saw her make an adjustment, using even more focused intensity, and with that "crack," the board broke. Delia was smiling ear to ear, and I could tell she'd just had a huge breakthrough. I took the broken boards to the front of the stage, held them over my head in a victory pose, and proclaimed, "What you just witnessed was an epic failure in board breaking!" The audience erupted with joyous cheers and applause!

They had been hearing about taking calculated risks, being willing to fail, failing forward, vulnerability, grit, and tenacity for three days, and now they got to see it live onstage. They had huge success in breaking their boards, so much so that we were able to finish on schedule. Many of the leaders stopped by to talk to me after the session ended, thanking me for the experience, which was nice. What really surprised me was the following email from the client:

"I want to reach out and thank you once again for the session you conducted at our Leadership Summit. I have spoken to several leaders who loved the experience and found it very empowering. I know with the elevation it wasn't ideal for you and your faculties may have been a bit compromised. Even so, you went with the flow and handled your circumstances like a pro. You were able to roll with what was before you and helped all of us learn from the situation. I actually had a few people ask me if you not breaking the board was planned. Thank you for being a true professional."

How was I able to turn what should have been a colossal failure into a great success? I was well prepared and stayed focused on the goal. Before my presentation began, last-minute changes were happening, and I had a choice on how to handle it. I could have gotten angry with the client and event producer, lashed out, and complained about them not being fair to me, and not adhering to the contract, but what would that have accomplished?

Attitude is such an integral part of success, and I chose to not take the changes personally. There was no advantage for me in thinking they were doing this to me on purpose, to harm me or to make my work harder. Their success was hanging in the balance with each change as well, so I was determined to do whatever was possible to help them succeed. That's what leaders do. We were all doing our best in this situation, and in the end we pulled it off—together.

My accommodating attitude allowed my mind to be in a more resourceful state when I failed, when several "unexpected outcomes" occurred. I was not burdened by negative emotions as I worked. Can you imagine what would have happened if I had presented while suppressing anger or rage? Do you think I would have been able to instantly pivot to the next-best action while hindered with a negative mindset? Good planning and preparation are of no value if you don't have the state of mind to take advantage of it.

Preparation allowed me to access where to go next in my presentation as unexpected outcomes occurred. I knew the message the CEO wanted me to convey and understood his vision for the event. I knew my material. I knew my plan. My timing was calculated down to the minute, so when timing changes happened, I knew where I could make cuts. I didn't plan for my board not to break *three times*, but because of preparation and focus on the outcome, in an instant I was able to use everything that happened to teach a lesson tied into the CEO's vision of bravery.

Staying focused on the goal helped me rapidly determine the next step. The ultimate goal was not for me to break my board as a form of entertainment; it was to get the company's leaders to break their boards and achieve their breakthroughs. Focusing on what I needed to do to help them reach their goal helped keep me from getting emotionally involved in the process, and you see how easily that could happen when you fail in front of hundreds of people.

Sometimes we take so much comfort in knowing we have a plan that we can become rigid, behaving as if it is the only way. As failure after failure happened on stage, live with no possibility of do-overs to save face, I took advantage of the opportunity for more in-depth teaching of the CEO's points on brave leadership. When Delia broke the board, I used that to show how leaders don't have to have all the answers. They can win by turning over the spotlight to let others step up to the challenge, helping them grow in the process. They learned about acknowledging failure, persistence, and never giving up. So much good stuff happened on the fly because I knew my material, I knew myself in my work, and most importantly, I was flexible enough to find ways to achieve our goals.

Do I wish I had broken my board on the first attempt? Absolutely! Is there anything more I could have done to be more prepared? I don't believe so. Do I consider this event a failure? No way. I actually rank this presentation as one of my greatest successes. To fail and recover so spectacularly that some of the leaders thought it must have been staged is proof that the message was well delivered and well received. This was a great day at work!

In the spirit of Thomas Edison, I endeavor to learn all I can from every unexpected outcome. A few hours following my presentation, I discovered canned oxygen at a little mountain store. It gave me instant relief from my altitude-sickness symptoms, and now I have one more thing to add to my preparation when I work at high altitude. I learned that Delia could rise to the challenge and perform under pressure. And I learned there are times when failure is not an option, not because I can't fail, but because I refuse to accept failure.

The difference between achieving success or failure can rest in something as basic as your attitude. You are the one responsible for the attitude you bring to all your endeavors in your personal and professional life. A positive attitude can go a long way in helping you achieve your goals and attracting others who will help you get there. So much of what we accomplish in life is a group effort, so learning not to take things personally will help you make gains. Anyone can lose their cool when under immense stress or pressure, so when others lose their temper, it is important to remember that it often has nothing to do with you. Don't let it affect your attitude. Thick skin is a useful asset when pushing through challenging situations with others and will help you stand out as an unflappable leader.

Although it is impossible to prepare for every single thing that can go wrong, the more prepared you are, the more resourceful you will be when it's necessary to make adjustments. No one knows you better than yourself, or what you need to do to feel ready for your next challenge. If you get well-practiced in preparation and are willing to be courageous in the face of small failures, you will grow to be able to handle any situation. Eventually, you will be able to handle anything, because you will be focused on success and nimble enough to respond to unexpected outcomes.

When you fail to meet a client or customer's expectation, you have an opportunity to create a raving fan and a customer for life with how you respond to failure. Reacting with defensiveness, or toxic emotions, will rarely lead to a successful outcome. When you have the ability to acknowledge where you fell short and take steps to remedy the situation, you are letting them know how important the relationship is. Just like my client at the ski resort, people do notice when you go the extra mile to exceed their expectations.

As you strive to achieve new successes in life, will you respond courageously in the face of fear of failure or will you retreat to the comfort of your status quo? You will surely experience failures along your journey, but you can let them refine you rather than define you. You can take your work seriously without taking yourself too seriously. Know yourself, know your stuff, have a plan, stay focused on your goal, and you can exude grace under pressure—helping you turn epic failures into great successes!

When we are no longer able to change a situation, we are challenged to change ourselves.

— Viktor Frankl
Austrian Holocaust survivor, neurologist, psychiatrist

CHAPTER ELEVEN

Overcoming Limitations

Since the beginning of time, people have overcome unimaginable obstacles and hardship to achieve success. We've heard stories of those forced to leave their country because of famine, religious persecution, or war. Some are survivors of terrorism or violent crimes. Warriors return home after experiencing the horrors of battle. There are children growing up in the foster-care system, being shifted from family to family dozens of times before adulthood. Prisoners have been unjustly incarcerated for decades for crimes they didn't commit, before finally being proven innocent with new forensic technology. It is impossible to create a list of all the obstacles and limitations a human being could face—and daunting to think about as well.

Many of us feel at some point in life like giving up, no matter the obstacles we face. Yet history shows us many people do overcome, tenacious in their pursuit of ways to transform what could be life-long limitations into just a part of their life's journey, and sometimes not even the most fascinating part.

I met one such person by chance at a local firewalk seminar. As we were preparing, I noticed a woman on the front right side of the room seated in a motorized wheelchair. Her service dog was obediently seated on the floor beside her. From the look of her gray hair, I would guess the woman was in her late sixties to early seventies, and while we have had countless people sixty to seventy years of age firewalk, this was the first to attend in a wheelchair. I asked Karen to go check with Doc, the doctor who was hosting the event on her property, to see what she could find out about this woman. Karen returned to tell me that Jackie was a friend of Doc's, who happened to be in town and wanted to attend. Doc also told Karen not to worry; Jackie was only there to watch.

I began as usual, with board breaking. When the boards were being handed out, Jackie was expecting a board, and Karen or I must have communicated to her that we understood she was only there to observe. I didn't notice, but over the next few minutes, Jackie had gotten out of her wheelchair and walked into another part of the building. All of this escaped my notice until I saw Jackie walk in from the back of the room. As she sat back down in her wheelchair, I saw Doc appear in the back of the room, smiling at me and announcing loudly, "Jackie can do whatever she wants!" Knowing nothing about this woman up to that point, I then learned something very important. No one tells Jackie what to do!

With our new understanding, Jackie quickly became part of the group. Participating full out, she rose from her wheelchair and broke her board with her bare hand. I remember that she wrote her empowering belief on her board: "I am free and strong." She broke her arrow with the soft part of her throat and encouraged others in their breakthroughs. I saw the can-do spirit of this woman, and others in the room saw it too. Amongst the participants was a group of about fifteen young men from a residential addiction-treatment center, who were learning to live with their own disease of addiction. This made for a diverse group of people with obvious, and inconspicuous, limitations to overcome in life.

During a break, I learned from Doc that Jackie was sixty-nine years old and had been diagnosed with myasthenia gravis, a rare autoimmune neuromuscular disorder that caused weakness in the skeletal muscles. At any moment, her muscles could just give out, causing her to collapse. Jackie had lived an adventurous life, hiking the entire Appalachian Trail, not once but twice. The second hike was *after* her diagnosis. Those are amazing feats! It takes five to seven months for an able-bodied person to hike the 2,100 miles of trail from Georgia to Maine. When her symptoms became too severe, she retired from her career as an ER nurse and spent her time traveling in her camper, visiting her children and friends and exploring nature and the great outdoors.

When it came time to walk on the fire, Jackie drove outside in her wheelchair, service dog, Wabi, walking beside her. I walked first, and then one by one, others took their turn. Standing barefoot at the edge of the coal bed, they stepped onto the red-hot glowing embers, transforming all that previously held them back into confidence and power. Knowing what Jackie's condition was, I just assumed she would not be firewalking, but once again, I had underestimated Jackie. After about twenty people firewalked, Jackie took off her shoes and walked towards the front of the coal bed. Doc and a few others were holding Wabi back. Wabi, a golden retriever, was a full-fledged trained service dog, who would have walked on the fire right beside Jackie if left unrestrained. And I knew enough to restrain myself, having learned that, if Jackie believes she can do it, she can do it!

Jackie took her first step onto the coal bed. And then another step, followed by another. We all watched with great concern and anticipation, anxious for her to get off the fire, while cheering her on simultaneously. With every step, her dog strained to run to her master. When both feet were off the coal bed, Jackie's body collapsed, falling onto the dewy grass. Fellow participants gasped, thinking she had burned her feet. With what I had learned about her condition, I knew her feet were fine. I was right; they were perfectly fine. Jackie's body had supported her through her next adventure, and when she was safely off the fire, it gave way.

My friend and fire-tender John, not knowing Jackie had myasthenia gravis, ran to help her, thinking she was terribly injured. I ran over to stop him, letting him know she was fine. Jackie, being a fiercely independent woman, yelled for Wabi, because her dog was the best suited of all of us to help get her onto her feet. Once Wabi got Jackie back into her wheelchair, Jackie's legs spasmed for the next twenty minutes or so. From her calmness and unconcern, I could tell she had encountered this before and was aware of what her body would go through before returning to her new normal.

We had just witnessed another awe-inspiring feat by a woman for whom life was not a spectator sport—never had been and never would be. Although Jackie's body could no longer hike days of mountain trails, her spirit longed for another challenge. She had decided to test herself with a different kind of walk. A walk much shorter but one that would still enable Jackie to feel alive, because she thrived on doing, learning, and growing.

When it was time to say goodbye to all the newly minted firewalkers, I saw something heartwarming. The group of young male addicts made their way over to Jackie, and one by one, each shared their gratitude for her inspiration, with hugs, kisses, and words of encouragement as they said their goodbyes. Jackie had touched them, not with her words but with her action.

Jackie stayed behind, and my team and I had a chance to spend some time getting to know her. I shared that I saw what happened with the young men, and Jackie seemed genuinely confused by the whole interaction. She couldn't understand what the big deal was and why they would be so affected by seeing what she did. What was the big deal? The big deal was that spending a few hours with Jackie helped them put their own limitations into perspective and gave them hope that they too could live a full life. But to Jackie, she was just being herself.

Jackie taught me a lot too. When I saw her wheelchair and service dog, I thought she was just there to watch. While I first looked at her, I saw limitations; Jackie saw none. She knew what she was capable of and would not allow others to put their limitations onto her. Early in the evening, when she left the room to give Doc a piece of her mind, she fought for her right to participate, and she shouldn't have had to. That lesson will stick with me for the rest of my life. It made me aware of, and on the lookout for, my own unconscious biases.

When Jackie decided to walk across the coal bed, this was not the action of a reckless woman. She was not careless, or impulsive, and she had nothing to prove to any of us. In that moment, she was living on purpose, and her purpose was adventure, as it often had been. If asked, many of us would have recommended, for the sake of safety, that Jackie not firewalk. In actuality, this would have been more for our safety and comfort than Jackie's, and to her detriment. So often our first instinct is to put limitations on others to keep them safe, especially the young. This is counterintuitive, because growth doesn't happen without a certain amount of risk. Sometimes the risk will be physical, like firewalking, and other times it might be emotional, like risk of rejection. It is vital not to put our limitations onto others, and notice how we limit others without even realizing it.

In life, we will all experience limitations. Without a crystal ball, we never know what life is going to put in front of us in the way of limitations that are out of our control. Yes, there could be a sudden health crisis involving acute or chronic illness. Maybe a downturn in the economy that effects our income and the viability of our business, causing financial hardship. Losing a loved one can feel like a black hole of grief that we fear we will never climb out of. The devastation of losing worldly possessions in a natural disaster can be heartbreaking. When facing any of the myriad of hardships in life, we get to decide whether our limitations will be permanent or temporary. Just like Jackie, we get to decide whether to overcome or not—whether to break through or not.

There is a huge market for movies and books about such human suffering and triumph, because we can all relate to having to overcome. Seeing aspects of ourselves in these stories, in print or on the big screen, helps us put our own limitations into perspective and inspires us in the process. Hardship in life is going to occur. There is never a good time for it, and some of us will get more than our fair share. But we have a choice as to whether we become bitter about the unfairness of life and feel victimized by our circumstances or carry on with purpose.

The hard truth is that you have limitations, but you don't have as many as you think you do. And most often you are dealing with self-imposed limitations, coming solely from within. You had no choice in the matter. Limitations were imposed on you from the time you were born. Restrictions were designed to keep you safe as a baby, and then to keep you under control as you grew older. You grew to the extent that your programming and beliefs allowed you to, and this created your comfort zone. Here you often feel safe and supported by your environment, the predictability of it, and those in it with you. And don't confuse comfort with desirability.

Your comfort zone could be an unfulfilling and dreadful place, but if it is what you've always known, you will find comfort within it, even as it provides no comfort at all.

As you desire to do more and have more in life, you are required to break through the limitations that are holding you in your present circumstances. Facing self-imposed limitations can often present more challenges to people than the sudden limitations of a health crisis. For one, a health crisis can be more obvious and can present a real sense of urgency to reduce suffering and promote healing. There is less time to vacillate between staying stuck and facing fear of the unknown, which can be painful place to be when facing a self-imposed limitation.

A self-imposed limitation will require some introspection and self-observation just to know what the limitation is and how it is affecting you. You're required to make a self-diagnosis. Although, if you have a "know it all" loved one or friend, they have probably given you clues about what you need to do to grow, which in itself can cause resistance to change.

You will need to muster some courage to move outside of your comfort zone in order to break through, but the rewards will be worth it and oftentimes immediate. I know I have an unusual career, not something other little girls growing up in my neighborhood went on to do. I was fortunate to have been exposed to some really outside-the-box kind of experiences. I had such limiting programming that I was forced, time and again, to make the decision about what I wanted to do and what I needed to break through to do it.

You don't always need to take big moves outside of your comfort zone to create results. Each time you embrace fear of the unknown, fear of change, fear of failure—whatever it is at the time for you—as you step outside of your comfort zone, you will grow.

It will change you. That is why the place just beyond your comfort zone is called your growth zone. Look for small things you want to break through and begin there. Over time, you will enjoy the success of breaking down your barriers of self-imposed limitations and find yourself looking for things to break through.

If you need some motivation to get started, think about all that you are missing out on by holding onto the limitations you believe exist for you. Think about how much fuller your experience of life can be if you decide to break through even a few of your small limitations. Which small courageous actions outside of your comfort zone can create big changes in your life? Do you believe that you can break through to achieve what you want in life? Remember, during Jackie's board break, she identified her empowering belief: "I am free and strong." Look what she was able to accomplish in the matter of a few hours following that. Your freedom and strength await you, if you are willing to spend more time in your growth zone.

Sometimes the most powerful lessons come from the most unexpected people. Jackie has one last lesson to teach us. The name of her four-legged sidekick was Wabi-Sabi (Wabi for short). In Japanese, "Wabi-Sabi" is defined as a way of living that focuses on finding the beauty within the imperfections of life and accepting, peacefully, the natural cycle of growth and decay.

The decay in our inner landscape is made up of the programmed fears and beliefs that no longer serve us. The beauty of them is that, at some point in our life, each limitation served a purpose, supporting us in some way. There is no need to hide them, feel shame, or pretend they don't exist. We must acknowledge and accept our imperfections and limitations in order to overcome them. In our natural cycle of growth, we will need to remove the decay to grow beyond our current existence. This work will be done outside of our comfort zone, and for this, we will need courage and grace.

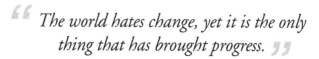

The world hates change, yet it is the only thing that has brought progress.

— **Charles Kettering**
American inventor, philanthropist

CHAPTER TWELVE

Fear of Change

Change is certain and ongoing. From the time we are born, we experience our body changing, rapidly at first, and then more gradually as we grow and develop through adulthood and into our later years. Once we learn to use our little legs, we are into everything, exploring with great fascination. Our vantage points of the world around us change as we grow taller. As children, we loath boredom, expecting our caretakers and life to constantly teach us something new. I remember my nephew Lee visiting my printshop as a little boy. He followed me around, wanting to model me doing the most mundane tasks. We would have to sit him in front of the computer and show him how to use the keyboard as a way to keep his little hands out of the running printing presses. Lee wasn't going to lose any little fingers or hands on my watch!

With this type of early life experience, you would think humans would gravitate towards change, especially at work. Although some people do welcome change, mainly as a way to break up monotony, a majority of people do not. So, what changed from embracing change—and dare I say, expecting it—and learning new things in childhood to bracing against the same in adulthood?

Our programming, that's what! Much of the programming of our childhood shaped our fears, beliefs, and perceptual filters, taking hold in adulthood and determining how we now experience our world. Our habitual behaviors over decades, driven by our programming, has reinforced our beliefs in the way things should be, and our fears when they are not.

Many of us have strong opinions about how our work life should be. We interview with a company or organization, accept a position, are told what our job entails, and then we are taught new skills for the job. We put our head down and get to work. In the beginning, we spend much of our time in the growth zone, navigating our role within the new environment, getting to know our way around and the new people we work with, learning new skills and applying ones already mastered. Spending so much time in the growth zone is stressful, but it is required to learn the new job. We strive to excel, until eventually, we are good at our job. It comes so easily to us that we can practically work on autopilot. We've earned this with all the hard work we put in, and predictability is our reward. And then, out of the blue, someone or something comes along and makes changes to the job we worked so hard to perfect.

As a print-production director, I was fortunate to work in an environment that suited my introverted personality. I worked at an advertising agency with fewer than twenty-five employees. I had my own office, and most of my work with outside vendors was done via phone or email. When I occasionally traveled out of the office for press checks, I would interact with a limited number of people—a press operator or two, a production supervisor, and maybe the salesperson handling our company account.

I always loved working in the printing industry. There is an exactness to the work, and I found it very black and white, no pun intended. Colors match or they don't. It's the correct paper or it isn't. The pages are in the right order or they're not. There is no ambiguity in producing a tangible product.

The work was fast-paced, and I was always racing to meet deadlines. I worked closely with the design team and account managers, who often attended client presentations and meetings. Luckily for me, I didn't have to go to those high-pressure meetings. I was more than happy to work behind the scenes, doing whatever work crossed my desk. In the beginning, it was easy for me to feel overwhelmed, changing from a print-shop to an advertising-agency environment. A lot of my time was spent in my growth zone, or as I like to call it, my stretch zone, because it really did force me to stretch my capabilities to fill my new position. Within my stretch zone, I discovered some hidden talents, like proofreading. It makes sense. I got to look for things that were wrong or out of place and make them right. Sure, I spent some time in my panic zone too, like during my first firewalk the agency sent me to, but even that worked out well in the end.

After a few years, the work domain I created was predictable. I grew to be great at my job. I knew what caused stress and also knew the long hours involved in my work, but there was a certainty to it. I could see myself working in this job, with the people I had grown so fond of, forever. And then, without warning, it all changed.

Sometimes change comes and it will have a minor effect on the type of work we do, or how we do it. We may experience some initial fear of change or anxiety, which subsides as soon as we understand what needs to happen and why. Some changes are so minor that we might consider them, and those who brought them to us, nuisances. There are those rare times though where the change taking place is so enormous that few can make sense of it, much less help others understand their role within the change.

I encountered this on a sunny South Florida Tuesday morning, when I received a phone call from the owners of the agency. They were out of the office at a meeting and just got word from their accountant in New York that something big was happening. Prepare yourselves. At the same time, our creative director gathered the employees and announced that the World Trade Center buildings had been hit, and any military veterans who were upset could leave the office. I remember being annoyed by his invitation to leave. We had deadlines to meet. What was he doing? I would soon realize that he, being a Navy veteran, understood quickly that the United States was under attack. I wouldn't comprehend the enormity of the tragedy until I got home that evening to see the television coverage. Everything in the world changed on September 11, 2001.

In the days that followed, work continued, but it seemed to lack importance. How does one care about direct-mail campaigns selling hotel rooms or bank credit cards when the entire world is in shock? One week later, as we were still trying to wrap our heads around what was happening in the business environment, anthrax biological weapon attacks started to occur via the U.S. Postal Service. Americans living in a state of terror from the September 11 attacks were now warned against opening mail, for fear of exposure to a deadly anthrax powder being mailed in letters. We were all scared, and rightly so.

Our clients immediately put existing direct-mail campaigns on hold. With citizens afraid to open mail, this would prove to be a prudent business decision. With the continued uncertainty of consumer and business trends, for obvious reasons, future campaigns were canceled. My work life, once so predictable and rewarding, was now slowly dissipating with each co-worker that was let go. There might be no crying in baseball, but there can be real sadness and grief at work when you lose aspects of your job that you enjoy, and people you've grown to love. Within a year, a once-thriving agency was shuttered, leaving each of us to deal with our own fear of change or excitement for the future.

I had time to plan my next move. After a few more years free-lancing in the printing and advertising industry, I decided it was time to make a big change. The firewalk that I'd been terrified to attend alone just a few years earlier had created significant change within me, and I found myself willing to take more risks and face my fears. I saw value in the experience and wanted to help others transform themselves with firewalking too. I was young enough that, if things didn't work out, I could always fall back into my old career, so I decided to follow my heart and teach people to walk on fire. I say "follow my heart" because there was nothing in my head that would have considered this to be a good idea.

Working with people to create change for themselves was diametrically opposite to my entire work experience. My work changed from the tangible—producing a product—to the intan-gible, working with people's emotions, feelings, fears, beliefs, and patterns to help them create change. While my previous career allowed me to tap into my natural talents, I was forced to uncover and also cultivate new skills and talents to fill the role of my new career.

My work environment changed from sitting at my desk, talking to one person at a time, to being on stage talking to hundreds of people. Instead of people trusting in the name of the agency I worked for, I needed to get them to trust me personally, especially to be willing to follow me onto the red-hot coal bed. I traded the predictability of machines for the unpredictability of people. I had to learn to use inspiration, compassion, and empathy instead of a ruler and computer. Where once I looked for the things that were wrong or out of place, I learned to help people see what was no longer working for them, never making them wrong in the process. Focusing on the smallest of details was now replaced with understanding the big picture of a company's goal or a person's purpose. There was nothing black and white about the new work I would be doing.

There is nothing black and white in the business world. Whether a business is a long-established brand or a start-up with a trendy new gadget or service, change is going to happen, and there is often nothing that can be done to stop it. Economic and market trends influence business projections. Events happening half a world away can force changes in the way we do business here at home. Geopolitics and international developments can create a volatile landscape for trade and technology. Natural disasters can disrupt entire regions and industries.

With the world constantly changing, big and small businesses are in a state of flux trying to stay ahead of the curve, leaving workers to find their place in the change. Experiencing change at work can be a psychological stressor. It doesn't matter whether the change is large or small, initiated from an outside source or voluntary, change can trigger a ton of emotions like anxiety, anger, fear, sadness, frustration, denial, and grief, just to name a few. Our resistance to change is a normal reaction, in an attempt to avoid the emotional toll. And yet, the resistance to change could be the very thing holding us in our own emotional stew.

We can break through our fear of change the same way we break through our other fears and limitations. Once we understand what is behind the feelings and emotions we experience when faced with change, we will be able to consciously take action to break through our own resistance.

Things changing at work can leave us with a sense of loss of control, especially when it is initiated from the powers above without our input. It is reminiscent of the retort, "Because I said so, that's why!" many of us heard in our childhood. Not only can we not control the change happening or the source of the change, but we also cannot control our emotions in regard to the change. This can create a really scary experience, but it is not hopeless, or a permanent condition. We might not be able to *control* the specific changes or the emotions they stimulate, but we can *manage* both.

The first step to managing fear of change is to realize that, oftentimes, change is happening to our job, and we just happen to be the one doing the work. This helps us not to take things personally. Engaging too personally can leave us feeling the need to defend our beliefs, if we perceive that the changes are unfair, unnecessary, or onerous, and can even leave us in denial that any change is going to take place at all. Yes, the way we do our job may be changing, but a sure-fire way to engage a mess of negative emotions is to personalize the change as something being done "to us," rather than to the job itself.

Keeping the amount of change in perspective is useful in managing our emotions while we come to terms with the fact that it is taking place. How much of our actual work is changing? Is it five percent? Ten percent? When the agency I worked for tried to implement use of software to manage projects and costing, the employees rebelled and dragged their feet learning the new system. Our collective belief was that we already had too much work to do and this was just going to slow us down. In the beginning, it would have definitely added to our workload, but over the long-term, it would have streamlined processes and made us more efficient and profitable. It was probably a 5 percent change in the work we did, but we were too defiant to see the benefits.

Sometimes anger gets the best of us when we undergo big change in the workplace. We might even feel like we are being set up to fail, which is rarely the case. If enough employees fail, the company will fail. Often, what our anger is masking is our own fear of failure. When faced with a lot of change, we can feel a deep sense of uncertainty. We wonder if we will be able to successfully carry out all our new duties. The change can be so great that we are unsure of the outcome.

This would be an opportune time to put some of what Thomas Edison taught us in chapter nine about failure into practice. A great reminder to ourselves is that, although we don't like to fail, we do like to learn, and if a large percentage of our job is changing, we'll have a lot of opportunity to learn. Because we have to "learn" before we can "do," we need to cut ourselves some slack and acknowledge that F.A.I.L. stands for First Attempt In Learning.

We may not realize it, but if we lose some of our favorite parts of our job, we can feel a deep sense of loss. Our identity can even be tied to what we do at work, so we have to give ourselves time to grow into our new role and accept what we lost in the transition. The same can be true for replacement of co-workers. We create a strong connection to others as we work together to build trust, solve problems, achieve goals, and support each other. It is natural to feel sadness or grief in the separation from (or loss of) people we have spent so much time with. To accept change at work, we need to acknowledge our loss and grief, and then let go of the way things were.

Not all change is bad, and some change will actually improve our work environment a great deal, if only we can get over our opposition to it. When you understand all the emotions, feelings, and fears wrapped up in change, it's easy to see where our aversion to change comes from. Most of our discomfort will not come from the outer experience of change itself, but from within ourselves and our emotional reaction to the change.

How do you handle change at work? Do you overreact, express anger, and maybe even sabotage the efforts of yourself and others? When asked to change the way you do something, do you assume your work is being criticized? Are you a victim, always being treated unfairly? These are all emotional reactions, which will not show you in a good light to those you report to or your co-workers.

Change is going to happen. It's impossible to anticipate all the ways your job and career can change. Things can happen unexpectedly. You won't always know what is coming at you, so it is best to be prepared with a mindset that is receptive and adaptive to change. This mindset will allow you to respond rationally, rather than react emotionally. You will appear confident and in control of yourself as you adjust to your new circumstances.

If you can embrace change, and move enthusiastically through the process of change, you stand a better chance of advancing in your career. You do this by believing you are competent to handle the change coming your way and helping others through their process when appropriate. You may even need to create a new support system if you lost part of yours in a transition. Be aware of what your response is, because you might be missing out on opportunity otherwise.

Changes or transitions at work may mean you get to learn some new skills and be exposed to a new way of working. Aspiring leaders will take advantage of every opportunity to add new tools to their tool kit. Even working with different types of workers and personalities presents opportunities to improve your people skills. If you are presented with the opportunity to do something way outside your usual work, take advantage of it. If you're lucky, you just might discover hidden talents that could have escaped you for a lifetime if not for this opportunity for growth.

You can benefit from change at work by seeing it as an opportunity for personal growth. Every time you get a chance to break through fear or self-limiting beliefs, you are creating change within yourself at a deep level. Sometimes you are put in a position where you are forced to disrupt a limited way of thinking, and breaking through fear of change is an excellent way to do this. How incredible to be able to empower yourself by being courageous at work!

Leaders have the crucial responsibility to lead others through change, while often in the midst of experiencing it themselves. Although not everyone you lead will experience every emotion, feeling, or fear mentioned in this chapter, if you lead a large group of people, you are likely to encounter them all. You can't control how others respond or react to change, but you can help alleviate some of their fears and concerns.

When people get word of change coming, their initial thoughts will be around job security. We like to feel we are in control of our own destiny, and the thought of changes in our work life can throw us off balance. The best way to help workers adapt is by giving the reason for the change, who is initiating it, what the expected outcomes are, and their role in it. When no information or reason is given, workers are left to fill in the blanks with their own imagination. Not being privy to the big picture that upper-level leadership has, workers will often catastrophize the meaning of what is taking place. Sometimes you will only be able to give limited information, but assuring them that you are telling them all you are permitted to, and that more information will be coming, is better than a "my way or the highway" message.

Most people are creatures of habit, thriving in predictability. Change forces your workers outside of their comfort zone and into their growth or stretch zone, which will bring up different levels of fear and feelings. Your job will be to help them overcome any barriers they encounter in learning their new roles. Too drastic a change, or someone in an inappropriate position, can send your people right beyond their growth zone and into their panic zone. This could have the disastrous effect of causing unnecessary frustration, struggle, opposition, and maybe even defiance to change.

Be willing to share from your own experience with change and address any vulnerabilities with support and encouragement. Help your team see value and their role in the change. Train your people well and put them in the best positions to excel at work, because most people don't want to be good at their job; they want to be great, and also feel great about the work they're doing. Leaders who can help their workers navigate change are worth their weight in gold and an asset to their company or organization.

In a perfect world, we would work only from our top strengths, and every day at work would be just like the one before it. Our favorite parking spot or seat on the train would always be waiting for us, and we'd be walking out the door right as the clock strikes quitting time. Fortunately, we're not robots, and the most successful people will find a way to take advantage of change.

This book was written during the great pause of coronavirus. Never in my life have I ever had the desire to write a book, but with the event industry and corporate meetings coming to a standstill, I had nothing but time on my hands—time available to do something new, difficult, and meaningful, and way outside of my comfort zone. This experience has been akin to discovering that, as an introvert, I can entertain audiences from the stage. This new way of connecting with people would have remained unknown had I not had the courage to face big change.

When life puts change in your path, it is an opportunity for you to make great things happen, if you are willing to take the risk of leaving your comfort zone. Be courageous in the face of change at work, and you could transform your career in unexpected ways.

---❖---

" *Yesterday I was clever,
so I wanted to change the world.
Today I am wise,
so I am changing myself.* "

— Rumi
*Thirteenth century Persian poet, scholar,
theologian and mystic*

---❖---

CHAPTER THIRTEEN

Changing Yourself

In the previous chapter, we talked about change that happens in the workplace. Workers looking to advance their career or improve their skills are more likely to be self-motivated to change. Changing to get the edge on the competition, or learning new skills to make the job easier, provides an incentive. Even people who don't really feel the need to change their behavior frequently will if their boss manages with the "change the people—or change the people" philosophy. In this case, risk of being replaced might be all the incentive that is needed to change.

When people are motivated to change on a personal level, we consider them to be seeking self-improvement, personal growth, or personal development. It doesn't matter what we call it; it's the concept of changing one's self that's important. Looking to improve our life is a virtuous endeavor that will require us to become aware of ourselves at a deeper level. The degree of honesty needed through this aspect of our growth is the biggest reason people stay stuck. It's scary to peel back the layers of all the masks we've created over our lifetime and see our true self—our most authentic self. It takes courage to expose ourselves to our deepest vulnerabilities and things we may not like.

Becoming aware is the first step in changing anything. We have to know what's working and what's not working in order to know what change will be beneficial. The process of introspection, self-observation, and soul-searching will help us develop our awareness. It seems like a lot, but once put into practice, it can become second nature.

Introspection deepens our understanding of our inner world and is an invitation to self-curiosity. Introspection helps us identify our <u>personality traits</u>, i.e., extrovert/introvert, optimist/pessimist, funny/serious, energetic/lazy, and our <u>character traits</u>, i.e., honest/dishonest, loyal/disloyal, generous/greedy, patient/impatient, courageous/cowardly. It also helps us examine thoughts, feelings, and emotions, and acknowledge strengths and weaknesses—and our reasons/motives behind the things we do. It also enables us to become aware of our barriers.

Self-observation is an exercise of paying attention to our thinking, feelings, and actions as they are taking place. It is extremely important to do self-observation in a non-judgmental and compassionate way, putting ourselves in the place of an outside observer, watching with no emotions attached to what we see and hear. This exercise allows us to objectively observe all that we identified about ourselves during introspection in action, and the effect that it all has on our life. This will help us identify what's working for us, and what's working against us. Remember, this must be done as if we are a neutral party watching from the outside looking in, making no critical judgment of self.

Soul searching enables us to decide how to move forward with our new, deeper understanding of ourselves and our values. As we create a vision for what we want our future to look like, it becomes clearer what needs to change, what we need to let go of, what we need to break through, and what we consciously choose to carry forward, in order to be successful.

Personal growth is not for the cowardly or shortsighted. Going through this process will reveal a lot of unpleasant situations or actions that we're currently engaged in, and those in our past that we regret or are embarrassed about. Even the saintliest person will have things they wish they could change about themselves, or things they wish they could go back in time and undo because of the harm it caused to themselves and others. The intention is not to beat ourselves up but to become aware of what's working and what's not working in our life, finding the patterns of behavior that are causing limitations, so that we can transform the patterns and break through the limitations.

Fortunately, not everything unveiled will be unpleasant. We will spot some real goodness in ourselves and our life. We'll notice things and areas where we've already grown and the opportunities that have opened up to us because of it. People seeking personal development are just speeding up the process by actively searching for things to change, in order to do more, be more, and have more in life. Whether it's more love, more money, greater connection to others, a willingness to take risks ... there is *something* you are inspired to accomplish, and you are ready to break through barriers to successfully achieve it.

Not everyone has an interest in personal growth. Some people are perfectly happy with where they are in life and see no areas in need of improvement. We might notice they are pretty much the same person they were ten or fifteen years ago, and not much has changed in their life, but they will be genuinely happy for our growth and success.

If they are cynical and feel threatened by our growth and new areas of interest, they might actually be afraid of change, ours and theirs. They could be afraid to change themselves, thinking it is impossible or too hard and not worth the effort. They might also be afraid of losing us if they don't change—too afraid to change, and yet afraid of growing apart. If they are an important person in our life, like a spouse or partner, this can be a really painful or frustrating experience. We can't force others to change, and the more we try, the more they'll resist, causing the separation to grow. If change is important to us, we must stay the course and hope they are inspired over time to create change for themselves. Sometimes giving up our attachment to someone else's personal growth will give them space to want it for themselves, which is truly the only way it will happen.

Fear of losing people in our life is a real risk that can cause us to stay stuck. If our goal is tremendous growth and change, it is inevitable that we will leave some others currently in our life behind. We must forge ahead bravely, trusting that we will attract other like-minded people as our world expands.

When we are committed to personal growth, change can happen quickly, with the next area to focus on improving often magically appearing. This happened to me very early on in my pursuit of personal development.

If you recall in the previous chapter, I wrote that we have strong opinions about the way things should be at work. Well, I am no exception. I was working in my job at the ad agency and found myself in a serious disagreement with my boss. We were inundated with work and deadlines, and I made the decision to clear a task off our design team's plate. A print vendor was going to create a die strike for a mailer, and my boss wanted our designers to do it. Standing in my office, I spent a few minutes explaining that the printer had included the die strike in our cost. It was not costing us an extra penny for them to do the work. There was no reason to have our design team spend more time on the project.

She didn't want the printer to create it and insisted that our designers do the work. Again, I explained that we had already paid for the printer to do it. We would surely miss a deadline on an unrelated project if this went back into our design department. She couldn't give a reason, except that we had to do it. It wasn't even that the printer would do it incorrectly, because they were pros. I could see no reason for this demand.

This back and forth went on for about ten minutes, growing so loud that we ended up closing my office door. We were both dug into our positions, both seeing ourselves as right. I worked with a lot of passionate people, but this was the most volatile situation I had ever found myself in at the agency. At some point, she ended up in the far corner of my office, with me in front of the door. By now it was heated. We were screaming at each other and neither was going to give in. In a rage, needing to physically release the energy of my anger, I turned around and punched my office door.

This brought our argument to an abrupt end. Both of us stood in shocked silence. My boss, small in stature, stood frozen, trapped in the far corner with no way out. Without a word, I opened the door and stepped aside, allowing my boss to make a quick exit. I could tell by the silence in the design studio and surrounding offices that everyone had heard our explosive argument. I apologized and retreated to my office, horrified and ashamed.

With my door closed, I sat at my desk, trying to compose myself and figure out what to do next. I noticed that the door did not have a hole in it, thank goodness. Instead, the many coats of paint on the seventy-five-year-old door had peeled off above and below the point of impact, but had not fallen off. Instead, the peeled paint formed many sharp fangs, each approximately ten inches long, curling outward off the door. My rage had produced what looked like a huge angry mouth. The metaphor was undeniable!

What was also undeniable were my anger issues. This obviously would become my next area of personal growth—learning to manage my emotions. My boss and I made amends and carried on as usual. The printer made the die strike, but I did not consider this a win. I lost a lot in this situation, like self-control and self-respect, and I also lost sight of my principles. With everything back to normal at the office, it would have been easy for me to rationalize my behavior, blame my boss for being unreasonable and making me so angry, but that route of action was no longer acceptable. Since I was committed to improving myself, I needed to turn this awful situation around, dig deep into myself, and see how I could transform self-defeat into personal gain.

Through quick introspection, I understood what it was within me that fueled this perfect storm. I was always quick to anger, even in my childhood. I was also very fearful, and anger is often a mask for fear. When we are in situations where it is not safe to show fear, we often unknowingly resort to anger. I was very competitive. I liked to win. I liked to be right. I hated to break promises. So, my fear of losing a fight, being wrong, and missing a deadline intensified my anger to a degree I could not control.

Now I had the reason for my behavior, and the thought of it happening again was intolerable. I replayed the office scene in my head, this time visualizing ways to handle the situation that was congruent with who I was striving to be as a person. Early on, I could have shown my boss the estimate from the printer, noting that the die strike was included, in black and white. If she still insisted on involving our design team, I could have shown her our production schedule and let her choose the project we would miss the deadline on. If I could not change her mind with reason, I would need to honor her position as the boss and carry out her decision, knowing I did all I could.

I wanted my values, principles, and actions to be in alignment, so I set on a course to break my pattern of reacting with anger, and to do this, I would need to be aware of when it was happening. I set out to practice self-observation, noticing when I found myself in disagreement or opposition with others. The earlier I caught it, the better. As I was involved in these interactions, I became skilled at watching myself from the outside and finding ways to disrupt my usual behavior.

Instead of feeding my need to be right, I would work to create win/win situations, so that no one walked away feeling defeated. This involved listening, flexibility, compromise, and negotiation. Years later, while giving an empowerment seminar at a South Florida jail, a prisoner shared a question he asks himself when he's in disagreement with others: "Do I want to be right, or do I want to be in relationship?" I now ask myself that same great question, although I do so with the understanding that the goal of creating a win/win is not always possible. We can't put ourselves in a position where we sacrifice our ethics or values, but an honest attempt at a win/win will disrupt our impulses to always be right.

I became adept at active listening to understand what others felt so strongly about and why. I felt less need to defend myself and my position or opinions. I grew to appreciate differences, instead of expecting everyone to be like me and see things my way. I would see value in influencing and persuading others, rather than using anger to force my way.

In an instance where I did feel intense anger, I noticed something funny. When I was feeling anger, but not engaging in it, I felt the tops of my ears burning as if there was a flame just about to touch my skin. This became a sign for when I was in a dangerous and unhealthy situation. Self-observation became so useful to me that I would only feel this intensity of anger a few more times before it never happened again.

My intention was to learn to manage my emotions, but doing the personal work helped me grow in other areas too, like communication with myself and others, patience, listening, appreciating diversity of thought and opinion, etc. Change happens quickly, because so much change can happen simultaneously.

An unexpected benefit of this one process in my personal growth was that it eliminated my anger at other drivers on the road, which some people might experience as road rage. This is saying a lot considering I drove the roads of South Florida then, and currently, Atlanta! If you do any kind of driving in densely populated areas, you've probably been on the receiving end of the anger I'm talking about.

Many years ago, my mother was driving in a shopping-center parking lot with my nephew Lee strapped into his car seat. As she was getting ready to pull into a parking space, another driver raced in and stole her spot. As she drove off to look for another space, Lee innocently asked, "Grandma, is that person an asshole?" It's funny, but in a way, it's not. He learned that somewhere. We owe it to the little ones around us to be the best version of ourselves, because they model us, even at our worst.

Are you interested in pursuing your own personal growth but don't know where to begin? Spend some time daydreaming about your future and notice what shows up. How far into the future do you see? Are you having exciting adventures? Exploring the world or staying close to home? Doing any interesting or unusual things? Are you alone or surrounded by lots of people? Are you advancing in your career? Going back to school? Finding love? Starting a family? Building a business?

Reflect on your current life circumstances. Is everything in your life the way you want it, or are there things preventing happiness and interfering with your goals? Any relationships that could use improving? Do you fear commitment? Would you like more confidence? Are there talents you would like to develop? Are you interested in increasing your emotional intelligence? Do you do things that cause conflict or disruption in your life? Does fear cause you to miss opportunities?

You will begin to become aware of things you'd like to accomplish, now and in your future, and realize there are some personal barriers you'll need to break through to achieve them. You'll notice how some of your behaviors are actually causing you stress or unhappiness, hindering the very things you want.

Difficult people and situations will also show you where you have personal work to do, so don't avoid them. The most difficult people in your life will often be your greatest teachers in your personal change. Those people who always seem to find a way to push your buttons are unwittingly showing you some of your opportunities for change. They will continue to push your buttons until the buttons (triggers) no longer exist. You do this by disrupting the patterns of your old programming until your buttons cease to trigger a reaction from within you. This might involve intentionally not engaging in an argument or biting your tongue while you listen to understand the other better. As you change and grow, so will the dynamics in your relationships. People around you will change without even realizing it.

Have you considered the reasons you want to change? What is inspiring you to change? Why is change important to you? If you have strong enough reasons, you are more likely to push through the tough times. You will find sources of motivation you didn't know existed.

I encourage you to begin a practice of introspection, self-observation, and soul searching, always from an objective place of nonjudgment and compassion. Refrain from being critical of yourself, because this will hinder you. Have the courage to be honest with yourself and open-minded about whatever you are becoming aware of.

Trust the process of change. Humans are creatures of habit, and there may be times you'll fall back into old patterns. Know that when stressed, whether at work or at home, you're more likely to default back to your old programming. It is your brain's primal response, returning you to what you already know, and it's important to refrain from beating yourself up when you do. When you become aware that you've resorted to old programming, this is actually your process working. Good job for noticing it. You are not your programing! Keep moving and growing forward, with your eye on progress, not perfection.

It is important to know that there are certain things you cannot change about yourself, no matter how much you would like to. Some of your personality traits are innate, like introversion or extroversion. As an introvert, I've learned to manage my energy when I am in the company of others and also know that I need alone time to recharge. Extroverts actually get energized by being with others. You also need to take things like genetics and mental illness into account. Someone suffering with anxiety might not be able to change from being a worrier, but seeking professional help may reduce the symptoms.

Be patient, with yourself and others. You will be excited to see results of your efforts and the new things your growth brings into your life. It is natural for you to want to share and bring others along with you. If change happens quickly for you, they may become threatened or distrusting of what is happening. You can't change other people, no matter how much you want it for them. Nagging doesn't work, and besides, it's annoying and irritating and will cause them to dig their heals in. Inspire them with your actions and success and give them space to grow. And be prepared to continue on if they don't.

You are now on your path of personal change. This is your journey, and you get to decide where to begin. Believe that change is possible, and that some of the changes you desire can happen quickly. I have spent years seeing people become aware of programming and self-limitations and break through them in the span of a few hours.

It is interesting how quickly something can shift just by delving into your emotions, feelings, and actions in regard to specific situations. When you can view your true self, without judgment and with compassion, you have an opportunity to become aware of your patterns, caused by your programming. Every time you take an action that is outside of your usual impulse to react in anger, or with another strong emotion, you are disrupting your programming. It is akin to taking your favorite DVD and putting deep scratches into the surface. It will continue playing the same movie, exactly the same way, over and over again, until the scratches occur. Once scratched, the DVD is no longer able to play the same movie. The programming has been disrupted—the pattern has been broken.

I have much evidence of this in my own life; that's why I know it is possible for you. I was hesitant to share the story of my explosive-anger episode with the world, but as I wrote it, I felt like I was writing about someone else. I have changed so much from that period in my life that it seems like a lifetime ago. So, if you are ever in doubt about whether change is possible and worth the effort, it absolutely is! Take it from me.

If you are afraid of change, I'll leave you with this thought: Change is going to happen. It's a constant in your life, and you often have no control over what it is and when it comes. Personal change is the change that you can control—whether to move into it or away from it. You get to control the pace and the depth. You get to decide your destiny. You get to decide how much your life and world expands. The question is this: Are you afraid to change? Shouldn't you be more afraid not to? Be courageous in your quest for change!

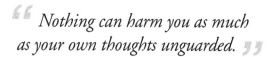

Nothing can harm you as much as your own thoughts unguarded.

— Buddha
Ancient Indian philosopher

CHAPTER FOURTEEN

Don't Believe Everything You Think

I've spent the previous chapters discussing fear and how many of our fears create barriers to our success, but there is something just as harmful that many of us never consider: beliefs—specifically, our self-limiting beliefs.

Self-limiting beliefs (negative beliefs) wreak havoc on our aspirations and happiness. I jest that self-limiting belief is fear's evil twin. They are both unseen, cause limitations from within, and will remain in the inner landscape of our mind until we eradicate them. There is one big difference though: Fear often presents with intense physical feelings such as a racing heart, perspiration, adrenaline rush, tingling in the extremities, dry mouth, dread, etc. Fear has an awful way of letting us know of its presence. A limiting belief is far more subtle. It's insidious, running just under the surface of our thinking and feeling.

Many of us move through life totally unaware of how our beliefs shape our experience of the world around us. We have beliefs about everything: money, love, success, religion, intelligence, leadership, failure, worthiness, UFOs, fairness, afterlife, work, family, war, freedom, loyalty, happiness, equality, ghosts, luck.... The list is endless. We have strong beliefs about things that are important to us, and beliefs about things we know absolutely nothing about, often unaware that we have such a belief or why. Our self-limiting beliefs are the ones that will create the most problems for us and rob us of our ability to make things happen.

In seminars, when I ask people, "What is a belief?" I hear answers like truth, fact, absolute truth. While it is accurate that we often behave as if our beliefs are true, many of them are not, especially our self-limiting beliefs. We are programmed with, and learn, many of our beliefs during childhood, and traumatic or stressful adulthood events, much in the same way our fears are programmed. When we are aware of our beliefs, we hold them as our truth, or as fact, because of the feeling of certainty that accompanies the belief. Strong opinions or beliefs held by other people can become our own, and we have no idea that it has happened. Many of our beliefs are carried deep in our subconscious, unknown to us, driving our behavior, thoughts, and feelings. Many of the self-limiting beliefs we carry around are false, and unfortunately, we have come to think and feel as if they are true and act accordingly.

I was facilitating an event for a group of high-level teenage athletes, whose coach was surprising them with an empowerment firewalk seminar during a training trip to South Florida. The kids were competing on a national level in springboard and platform diving, and this being one of my favorite Olympic sports, I was looking forward to meeting them.

The day before the event, I met with the coach, and he went over his roster of divers, telling me their ages and a little about what he thought each athlete's issue was. Fear came up a lot. It makes sense in a sport where a simple mistake can lead to a serious injury. I still remember Greg Louganis in the Seoul Olympics, hitting his head on a springboard, requiring four stitches, and then minutes later heroically nailing his very next dive. He would advance and go on to win the gold medal the following day. I imagine these young athletes have had their own share of close calls and hard knocks running through their minds.

As we worked our way through the roster, he told me about a fifteen-year-old girl who was a student at Harvard University. What? Wait a minute. THE Harvard University? I was already in awe of this girl and now super excited to meet the team. Tomorrow couldn't come soon enough.

We began the seminar with board breaking. I asked the athletes, coaches, and parents in attendance to identify a fear or self-limiting belief they needed to break through to reach their next level of success, and to write it on one side of their board. The room filled with cheering and encouragement as pairs came to the front of the room to break through their boards with their bare hands. Young thirteen to eighteen-year-olds were having breakthroughs, as well as some scared parents. As we wrapped up board breaking, I noticed a girl in the back row with tears streaming down her red cheeks. She had her unbroken board in her lap. I didn't point her out, because the activity was voluntary, but I could tell she was going through her own process of breaking through. She was not yet ready to break through her board, or maybe face what she had written on it.

We moved on to the steel-rebar-bending and arrow-breaking activities. I noticed the girl who was crying in the back row had gotten herself to a point where she could participate, and she was successful with both challenges. This was a great sign. A quick break and then we would all head outside the hotel to light the fire. During the break, a teammate sitting beside the girl who had been crying asked me, "My friend wants to break her board. Can she do it quickly while people are out of the room?" I told her yes, she can break her board, but we would need to wait until everyone was back. She agreed. I knew the crying girl was about to experience a huge breakthrough, and it was important for others to bear witness.

Once everyone was seated, the girl brought her board to the front of the room. On her board, she identified two self-limiting beliefs that were barriers to her success: "not smart" and "not worth other people's time." I saw her nametag, and suddenly, I realized this was the fifteen-year-old Harvard student. *If she's not smart, then I'm doomed!* I remember what I was doing when I was fifteen, and it didn't compare with her academic achievement. I could tell by the reaction in the room that everyone was shocked that she thought she wasn't smart. But this is the nature of our self-limiting beliefs. To us, they feel very true, factual, and accurate, but to others who know us, they are often illogical, unfounded, and nothing could be further from the truth.

It wasn't enough for me to say to her, "Come on, kid, you're at Harvard. You're smarter than all of us put together. Of course, you're smart! Get over it." I needed to help her challenge her *own* beliefs, and I did that by asking questions, literally questioning her belief in a way to help her create doubt about its validity.

Me: "Where do you go to school?"
Her: "Harvard."
Me: (Incredulous) "Harvard? Harvard University in Cambridge?"
Her: "Yes."
Me: "How old are you?"
Her: "Fifteen."

Me: (Amazed) "Fifteen! Are there a lot of fifteen-year-olds at Harvard?"
Her: "No. People are old there. They're in their twenties and thirties."

The parents and coaches erupted with laughter.

Me: (Puzzled) "Do they just let anyone into Harvard?"
Her: (Slightly annoyed by my ignorance at this point) "No. You have to score really high on the SAT. Acceptance rate is less than 5 percent. People there are really smart."
Me: (Confused) "Really? Is everyone smart there?"
Her: (Quick to answer) "Yes"
Me: (Slowly) "Interesting. Even you?"
Her: (Shrugging her shoulders, smiling) "I guess so."
Me: (Quizzically) "I guess so? Could I get into Harvard?"
Her: (Looks at me for a few seconds and proclaims) "Oh, no!" (shaking her head from side to side.)

The room filled with laughter at her wise crack, and I knew I was halfway there. I then had to challenge her belief that she was not worth other people's time. And this was like divine intervention, because we had a firefighter waiting outside for our fire lighting, and we were now running behind schedule.

Me: "What else do you have written that you need to break through?"
Her: (Looking serious again) "Not worth other people's time."
Me: "That's interesting. Do you know where we're supposed to be right now?"
Her: (A little confused) "No. Where?"

Me: "There is a firefighter outside waiting for us to come out and light the fire. He's been waiting for us for at least fifteen minutes now. What do you think we should do?"

Her: (After a few seconds) "Go light the fire?"

Me: (Speaking to the group) "Raise your hand if you think it's best to wait to light the fire for her to break her board." (Every hand went up. I could tell everyone was being very supportive, anxiously awaiting her breakthrough.) "How much time should we give her?"

Group: (Shouting out encouragement) "As much time as she needs." "We'll wait all night!" "You got this!"

Me: "I had no idea what was written on your board. Do you know why I was willing to run so far behind schedule?"

Her: "Because I'm worth it?"

Me: (Excited) "Exactly! You are definitely worth my time! Everyone in this room is supporting you and giving you their time too! How incredible is that?"

Her: (Looking relieved, she smiles.)

Me: "What new beliefs did you create for yourself, written on the other side of your board?"

She held up her board, and large across the top, she had written "CONFIDENCE," and underneath it, "I'm smart enough and worth it!" She had already had her breakthrough, looking more confident and secure within herself. She broke through her board powerfully. Clapping and cheering filled the room, and she got high-fives all the way back to her seat, smiling from ear to ear! She decided to burn her board in the fire and would later courageously walk barefoot across the hot coals with the confidence of a seasoned firewalker.

Beliefs drive everything! They determine how we think and feel about ourselves, others, and the world around us, affecting our emotions and our behavior. Do you need more evidence than seeing how a belief made a teenager at Harvard University think she lacked intelligence? Beliefs have a way of tricking us into thinking we are less than we actually are, less loveable, less intelligent, less beautiful, less talented, less worthy, less capable.... You get the point. This is why it is dangerous to believe everything we think!

I learned this for myself shortly after I became intentional in breaking through my fear. My very first self-limiting belief I became aware of was that I thought I was not smart enough. The bad news was I was twice the age of the Harvard student when I realized it. The good news? It was not too late to reap the rewards of believing in myself. It's never too late! I set out on a path to learn all I could about my beliefs and how they were affecting my life. I'll share with you the basics of what I discovered.

My first step was acknowledging that I had the capacity to break through my limiting beliefs, just as I learned to break through my fears. I would no longer resign myself to accept that "I am the way I am" or "this is just who I am." While it's true that there are some things that I can't change about myself, I had a lifetime of false-hoods to uncover—lies that had become my truth. It's intriguing that the word "lie" is right there in the middle of the word be*lie*f, a word signifying truth. It's as if belief is playing games, scheming and plotting against us with our self-limiting beliefs, yet leaving a clue for us to crack the code.

To crack the code of my beliefs, I needed to understand where they came from. Like fear, I started forming my beliefs at a very early age, before I was even aware that it was happening. I took on many of the values and beliefs of my parents and our culture, especially in regard to love, acceptance, right and wrong, religion, honesty, money, gender roles, and work ethic. Experiences and events shaped my beliefs. Schooling and gaining knowledge also formed my beliefs. My past successes and failures shaped my beliefs. I learned that having the same thought over and over again creates a pattern of habitual thinking that can create a belief.

When we are young, we have less ability to manage our thoughts, leaving us susceptible to other's opinions of us. Consider the difference in constantly hearing either of the following about yourself throughout your entire childhood: "You're never going to amount to anything" or "You can be anything you want to be." Hearing either of these statements regularly could lead to a pattern of thinking this thought over and over again, until eventually, it becomes a belief. The former belief would be extremely limiting, while the latter would not. A person who believes they can be anything they want to be is more inclined to have bigger dreams and take risks. If you believe that anything is possible, why not give it a try?

This leads to my next step in cracking the code of my beliefs. I didn't just have self-limiting beliefs, I had self-enhancing beliefs too. I would come to call these two types of beliefs my empowering beliefs (enhancing) and disempowering beliefs (limiting). As I discovered my beliefs, I classified them as either giving me power or taking my power. This helped me to see an advantage in going through this process, working towards self-empowerment.

It became obvious to me that, to improve the quality of my life and advance my career, I would need to increase my number of empowering beliefs while reducing the number of disempowering beliefs. I knew this was possible, because of how my mindset was changing with each fear I faced. Now I needed to make myself consciously aware of how the programming of specific beliefs were affecting my life. It was now time for me to discover my truth and quit maneuvering through life with harmful, disempowering beliefs dictating my feelings and actions.

Would you run your business or department using twenty, thirty, or forty-year-old data? Of course not! That would be career suicide. And what if some of the data is not just old but was faulty from the beginning! Why would you run your life with decades-old, faulty data? I'm here to tell you that you don't have to. You have the ability to upgrade your data, in this case your programming, to create a mindset that will enhance and expand your life. You no longer have to settle for the restriction and limitation caused by your disempowering beliefs.

Now is a great time for you to crack the code of your own belief system, no matter your age or level of success. Akin to fears, we all have a limiting belief or two that could keep us from achieving our next level of success.

Begin by taking inventory of your beliefs, empowering and disempowering. This will help you understand the data that's been driving you, and help you identify what would be beneficial to upgrade. On two separate sheets of paper, write "Empowering Beliefs" on the top of one, and "Disempowering Beliefs" on the top of the other.

Over the next few days, as you become aware of a belief, add it to one of these two lists. It is important that you do this type of introspection without judgment. Resist the urge to label things good or bad. Beliefs, just like fears, may have served a purpose for you earlier in life, or maybe weren't yours at all to begin with. Do you remember the spider story in chapter two, showing how you were programmed with other people's fear? The same is true of beliefs. What matters now is becoming aware of what is no longer serving you—what is actually obstructing or impeding your growth and success.

Self-talk, our inner dialogue, can alert us to what some of our beliefs are. Since beliefs drive our thoughts, we will often have habitual thoughts related to a belief. Actual words that we speak can also lead us to become aware of our beliefs. A great example of this is someone noticing they are constantly critiquing their actions or thoughts as stupid. "That was stupid of me to use the wrong credit card." "How stupid to forget to pack my make-up." "I can't believe I presented the wrong stats. He probably thinks I'm dumb!" "Big dummy! Why did you think she would say yes?" I've known people who spoke words like this to themselves out loud. Our beliefs leave clues. We just need to be determined with our introspection and self-observation in order to seek them out.

Becoming aware of situations where you feel uncomfortable emotions can help you identify beliefs. If you are uncomfortable at the thought of being alone, you might have a belief that, if you're alone, you'll be lonely or that you're unlovable. Or if you are hesitant to put yourself in for a promotion, even though you are more than qualified to do the job, you might have some disempowering beliefs about your abilities, money, and/or your worthiness.

To help you classify whether a belief is empowering or disempowering, following are examples of both. You might also be able to distinguish between the two by using your senses. Does the belief make you feel lighter or heavier? Does it pull your energy upward or downward? Closing your eyes, do you sense lightness or darkness? Empowering beliefs are positive beliefs, associated with success and possibility, so they may leave you feeling lighter and energized, with lightness around your being and an upward flow of energy. Disempowering beliefs are negative beliefs, associated with limitations and obstacles, which can leave you feeling heavier, depressed, or sad, and experience a downward flow of energy and darkness around your being.

Examples of Empowering Beliefs

I am more than my programming.

I am good enough.

I am strong.

I am a winner.

I am a good person.

I am smart.

Life is an adventure.

I can trust other people.

The world is a safe place.

My body is my temple.

I trust myself.

I am my own best friend.

It's okay for others to disagree with me.

I am worthy.

I deserve the money I earn.

All I need is within me now.

Examples of Disempowering Beliefs

My programming limits me.
I am not good enough.
I am weak.
I am a loser.
I am bad.
I am not smart.
Life is hard.
People are untrustworthy.
The world is a dangerous place.
I don't deserve to be healthy.
I can't be trusted.
I need someone in my life at all times.
Everyone tries to make me wrong.
I don't deserve a better life.
I have to work very hard for my money.
This is too much for me. I can't do it.

These examples are meant to help you get a sense of various beliefs, and how simply they can be structured, to help you in identifying your own. There are no right and wrong answers as you make your lists. The possibilities of empowering beliefs and disempowering beliefs are as unique and endless as we are as humans, so be open minded in your exploration.

If you would like to separate your beliefs as they apply to different areas of your life, you can create categories like career/work, relationships/family, money, self-worth, health, spirituality/religion, and so on.

Don't be concerned if your disempowering beliefs outnumber your empowering beliefs. I have found this is common when people begin the process of discovering their beliefs. And don't be overwhelmed if you end up with a long list of disempowering beliefs. Clarity is power, and this will give you more to work with. I found that, in doing my own belief work, just discovering that I had a certain belief was sometimes enough to release its hold on me.

As you compose your lists, you will already be in the process of upgrading your programming. In the next chapter, you will get to determine which of the old data you choose to replace, and how to transform your disempowering beliefs into empowering ones that work for you instead of against you. Be curious and nonjudgmental as you work to crack the code of your own belief system. And remember, don't believe everything you think!

" *We don't see things as they are,*
we see them as we are. "

— Anaïs Nin
French-Cuban writer

CHAPTER FIFTEEN

Change Your Beliefs;
Change Your World

Our beliefs determine how we perceive and relate to ourselves, others, and everything in our life. Our beliefs are responsible for creating the perceptual filters through which we experience the world around us. Things that are in alignment with our beliefs are more likely to enter our awareness, while things that are in opposition with our beliefs can remain hidden, elusive, or ignored.

A person with a long list of empowering beliefs (positive/enhancing beliefs) about themselves, others, and the world around them is more likely to have a positive outlook on life. Their perceptual filters allow them to see opportunities routinely missed by others, even in times of hardship or crisis, putting their skills and talents to good use. He or she will tend to be happier, more positive, and optimistic about their future. If we know someone like this, we might be left with the impression that they are just lucky, or that success comes easily for them. Happiness, joy, love, hopefulness, forgiveness, and trust will be more easily accessible for this person.

On the flip side, a person influenced by predominately disempowering beliefs (negative/limiting beliefs) will tend to be more negative about life and what the future holds. Their perceptual filters will be formed in such a way that shows them struggle, difficulties, and a lack of possibilities and opportunities. Instead of utilizing their skills and talents, they will doubt that they even exist or feel it won't make a difference anyway. Hopelessness, sadness, fear, anger, loneliness, and anxiety could be emotions frequently felt by a negative thinker.

In the previous chapter, we learned a lot about beliefs, including how to identify our own. If you have taken some time to become aware of your own beliefs, and composed a list of them, you might also have gotten a sense of how certain beliefs have affected not just the quality of your life but its trajectory. You are beginning to get an idea of the world your perceptual filters are allowing you to experience, created by your own beliefs, empowering and disempowering.

If this is your first experience in uncovering your beliefs, congratulations! Up until this point, you have been living under the conditioning (programming) of your early life. Undoubtedly, you have discovered some beliefs that you suspect are lies you have come to accept as truth. You now have an opportunity to beat belief at its own game, by isolating those beliefs that are holding you back and transforming them into beliefs that will propel you forward.

A few years ago, I sat in the audience at a corporate annual meeting, waiting to facilitate board breaking to close the event. The speaker right before me was an attorney and CEO who considered himself to be a servant leader of a community organization, overseeing an annual budget of eighty million dollars. He wasn't there to talk about finances, getting ahead, or leading with vision though. This very accomplished man spoke about how he was "not supposed to be there," because he once believed he was "not good enough" and "not talented enough."

His display of vulnerability was striking, as he stood in front of three hundred professionals and divulged things about himself that no one could have guessed. He shared his early life circumstances and the important people who worked hard to help him discover what he did have inside himself to be a success. Fortunately, at a young age, they saw the "good enough" and "talented enough" in him that he could not yet see. They pushed and supported him as he worked to get himself to exactly where he was meant to be, even if he didn't believe it. And as he shared his story, you could hear a pin drop, because everyone in that room could relate to the burden of hiding their own disempowering beliefs and struggling to succeed, while that voice in their head was telling them things like "you're not good enough" or "you don't deserve this."

I could really relate to this man's story, because years earlier, I had begun to explore my own beliefs. Once I learned I didn't have to accept my old programming from circumstances out of my control, I set out to rewrite my beliefs in a way that supported me. Some disempowering beliefs fell away as soon as I realized I had them, while others I would need to challenge, like I did with the teenage Harvard student. Below are some of my disempowering beliefs that were transformed into empowering beliefs, and also new empowering beliefs I created to support me:

I'm not smart enough → All the intelligence I need is within me now!

It goes without saying how much transforming this single belief can change one's life. At thirty-three years old, it was a game changer. I became much more at ease in my interactions with others, no matter their title or level of success. I wrote a list of all the successes I had in my life, all my accomplishments, and the things I had been able to learn. It was no longer possible to ignore the evidence once it was in front of me on paper. It is easy to brush aside information contrary to our beliefs, and we can thank our perceptual filters for that. Anything that doesn't match our belief gets disregarded as bad info. The change in feeling about myself, and my intelligence, was immediate and permanent. Challenging this disempowering belief led me to some other truths about myself, which also became new empowering beliefs: "I can learn anything I set my mind to." "If other people can do it, so can I."

Everything I do must be perfect in every way → I do my best and my best is good enough!

As a recovering perfectionist, this new empowering belief was freeing. Looking at everything one does as faulty or inferior can be soul crushing. I was able to end my pattern of being self-critical in the evaluation of my results. No matter what I am doing, work or play, I always give 110 percent, so I came to accept that, in that moment, that is my best. It is okay if I need to learn more in order to get better results. This new empowering belief helped me be more understanding of others and less critical of their results too. As a leader, I strive to bring out the best in my people, and when they fall short, it is my responsibility to give them the knowledge and tools they need to achieve better results. This led me to other empowering beliefs: "It's okay for me to make mistakes." "I learn from my mistakes." "All mistakes are learning experiences."

This one ties into Thomas Edison's view of failure. I strive to get better at something with every mistake I make: "When I know better, I do better." At this point in my life, I only know what I know, but I do like to learn, so I am always improving as I gain more knowledge.

I don't know enough → All I need is within me now!

This was a biggie when I changed my career from printing/advertising to facilitating empowerment events. I believed I needed a bunch of book knowledge that I did not possess and experience I did not have. What I needed to understand was that I had gathered my knowledge by living through my own self-empowerment process. I had everything inside me to help people already. There was no need to procrastinate any longer. As soon as I took the leap and started working, this proved to be true. This new empowering belief gave me a lot of confidence.

I have encountered many people who are going through the same thing, feeling they need one more degree or one more job title before they're able to make their next move or enjoy their success. Don't underestimate the knowledge you already hold, and the value of experiences you've already lived.

I'm not good enough → I am good enough!

This is one of the most common disempowering beliefs I see in my work. It can also be a tough one to break through. We live in duality, and everything exists within us. We cannot experience "I'm not good enough" without "I am good enough" also residing within us. This is actually true with all our beliefs. A dear friend of mine, who is also a therapist, describes it this way: If you have two plants to water, and one is vibrant and green and the other is withering, you are going to water the green plant first. This is the one that has been getting more of your attention, which is why it's flourishing. In terms of our beliefs, we need to make ourselves a priority and to water our empowering beliefs as opposed to the disempowering beliefs, which our primitive brain pays attention to in order to ensure our survival in the wilderness.

Somewhere along the way, you have come to accept that you are "not good enough," and that is what you have been giving your attention to for a very long time. You'll need to sit in silence and see if you can connect with "I am good enough" somewhere in your body. It is most often felt in the heart, gut, or solar plexus, located in the center of your torso a few inches above your belly button. Even if it is just a flicker or a spark of energy you feel or sense, it is in there. You'll need to make the conscious effort to feed "I am good enough" until it flourishes, leaving the other "I'm not good enough" to wither and die. When we are aware, we get to choose which one we nurture.

Change is impossible → I have the power to change things in my life!

This entire book is about breaking through barriers to create change in your life, so it is vital to believe that change is possible. I created many new empowering beliefs about change in my own life, such as "I trust the process of change." and "It is okay for me to change." These next ones are important, if you have people in your life who are resistant to you changing and growing:

"I am patient as I create change in my life." "I am ready to change." "I embrace change with grace and ease."

I have no control over my life → Everything happens for a reason!

This belief gives me a more peaceful feeling, as I gave up the illusion that I could control everything happening in my life. I don't have to know the reason for each and every thing that happens; I just need to trust that there is a reason for it, even if I am not aware of it at that time. I've had lots of things happen that seemed bad or unfortunate at the time, only to realize (at a later date) that it had led me to meet someone or encounter an opportunity I would have missed otherwise.

I've just given you some of the personal beliefs that I have changed, and the transformations they have led to. Did you happen to notice what I *didn't* do in the process? I didn't spend time going through my past, assigning blame or looking for reasons for each disempowering belief. There are two reasons for this: The first is that many of my beliefs were formed when I was so young that I was not aware it was happening. The second is that it *doesn't matter* where the belief came from; it only matters that I know whether it is giving me power or taking my power.

I have no idea why I believed I was not smart enough. I can't recall anyone of importance calling me stupid or insinuating I was unintelligent, and that's my point. What really matters is what your beliefs are keeping you from attempting, accomplishing, or feeling, not where they come from. I know for certain that I would not have made my career change or been able to write this book without first becoming aware of, and changing, this disempowering belief.

How are your disempowering beliefs holding you back? No one knows better than you what is going on in your head as you pursue your goals. Now it's time for you to begin changing, or shall I say upgrading, your programming, so that it is working for you rather than against you.

Now that you are aware of some of your own disempowering beliefs, you're going to need to create a new empowering-belief statement to replace each of them. Follow the steps below to create the most effective beliefs possible, in order to positively affect your subconscious programming:

1. **Stated in first person** – This is your subconscious programming, so take ownership of the belief. First-person beliefs begin with "I" or "My," or include "me," "myself," or "my."

2. **Stated in present tense** – You are rewriting your subconscious programming, not creating a wish list, so write it as if it is already true in this moment.

Here are some examples of present-tense, first-person belief statements:

"I am my own best friend."
"I am a dedicated employee."
"It's easy for me to learn new things."
"It is okay for me to set boundaries."
"My body is my temple."
"When I stay focused on my goals, anything is possible."
"I have everything I need within me to be successful."

Belief statements should <u>never</u> include "I want to..." "I'm going to..." or "I will..."

3. **Stated in the positive** – You want to focus on what is true, instead of what you don't want to be true, i.e., "I am a confident presenter" is more effective than "I don't want to be a nervous presenter."

4. **Meaningful** – You know what you are breaking through or moving towards, so use words that are emotionally meaningful to you. You want your new belief statements to have an impact on your subconscious, so make them invigorating!

   "Life is an adventure."
   "My heart is overflowing with gratitude."

5. **Keep it short** – It is easier for the subconscious mind to process a short belief statement. Five to ten words in length is best.

   "I accept myself."
   "I love myself."
   "I am a winner."
   "I am a good person."

Remember, you aren't required to have a disempowering belief in order to create a new empowering belief. If you identify some empowering beliefs that will help you achieve success, incorporate them into your subconscious programming.

Now that you have created new empowering beliefs, you want to disrupt your existing programming and override it with what you know to be true about yourself. Essentially, you are inputting accurate, current data into your programming—information that is a reflection of your true self!

Work with one belief at a time. I like to do this with physical activity, which is why firewalking and board breaking can be so effective in helping the new belief take hold. This enables the belief to become integrated into your mind *and* body, for a sense of whole knowing. You can use any physical activity from walking, running, cleaning, or a repetitive physical move like a victory pose or power move. Repeat your new belief in your head and/or out loud, over and over again. You can even give it a cadence to create your own motivational chant. Enjoy the energy that comes from the truth in your belief statement, and feel it in your body. Over time, you will build your new empowering belief, causing the disempowering belief to dissipate or minimize its hold on you.

You can create your own positive affirmation using your new empowering belief. You can write your new belief on Post-it Notes and place them in several places where you will see them throughout your day—your mirror, computer, refrigerator, and car dashboard. Give this new empowering belief the attention it deserves. Feel the energy and the truth of this belief statement in your body, as you think it and say it, starving that old false belief.

If you have a meditation practice, you can also incorporate your new empowering belief in the form of a centering thought or mantra.

Have fun and be creative as you incorporate your new empowering beliefs into your life. You may even discover other ways to implant your new empowering beliefs into your subconscious mind. As you use your conscious thought and conscious activity to work with your new empowering beliefs until they become natural, know that you are also reshaping your perceptual filters, literally changing and expanding your world as you live it!

> " *You cannot swim for new horizons*
> *until you have courage*
> *to lose sight of the shore.* "

— William Faulkner
American Writer, Nobel Prize laureate

CHAPTER SIXTEEN

A Story of Inspired Courage

There was once a little girl growing up in a faraway land. The terrain was large and plentiful, green with trees and covered with abundant crops and animals to feed its people. The little girl, named Constanzia, lived in a clan alongside countless other clans that inhabited this wondrous place.

Constanzia would grow up like all the other little ones, staying within her clan, learning its ways and customs, and what was expected. Being a good little girl, wanting to please her elders, she took everything in like a sponge. She knew the ways of her people well.

As she grew older, Constanzia would disappear for long periods of time. Since she was known as a dreamer, her clan just assumed she was off with her goat somewhere, lying in a field, wasting her time daydreaming. No one suspected her curiosity was leading her to venture out, secretly meeting others and observing differences in their ways.

On one such adventure, she and her little black and white goat named Dodger wandered so far from home that she ended up at a place she had only heard of in cautionary tales. The soil ended at the water's edge, from which the water went so far away it touched the sky. The water would come towards her and then run away, making a loud sound unfamiliar to her. People from other clans were in individual wooden containers, magically suspended as they moved farther from land.

As Constanzia stood in awe, with eyes and mouth wide open, feeling her heart pounding in her chest, an old man appeared by her side. "Are you okay? You look like you need to sit down," he said in a raspy voice.

"Yes. No. I mean, yes, I am okay." Breathless, her questions came fast and furiously: "Where am I? What is this place? How are they able to do that? What are those wooden things?"

He laughed. "Slow down, young one. Have you never heard of the sea before? There's a whole world out there, even beyond what you can see, but you have to go get it. It won't come to you. Those who want more build a boat out of trees and set off to explore it for themselves. They come back with great stories about their explorations, sharing with others what they learned and things they've found."

"But how can that be? I was told that nothing good happens here, only danger and heartbreak. In my clan, they say it is not for people like us," Constanzia said sadly.

"Well, I don't want to say your people are wrong, but your people are wrong. I have seen all types of people venture out to sea, young and old, male and female. And they all had two things in common: something they wanted and the courage to go get it."

"I'm so confused. I always sensed there was more to life than what I had been told, but now that I see it, I am scared and doubtful. What if it's true that it's not meant for people like me?" she asked with tears in her eyes.

"Well, there is only one way to find out. Think about what you want to do. I am very old, and you have much to learn, so I will send someone here to this very place in seven days. They will be able to help you discover your truth, if you are willing."

With that, Constanzia thanked the old man and gathered Dodger, who had been chewing a hole in the back of the old man's sweater. As they walked away, he yelled to her, "One more thing: Once you discover your truth, there is no going back."

Constanzia and Dodger ran all the way home, filled with excitement and possibility, but she would need to contain herself so as to not let on what she was up to. This would be the longest seven days of her life. During the first few days, her daydreaming reached new heights, thinking about what could be. But then, as more days went by, she started to feel her usual doubt and fear when thinking about leaving her little village. And what did the old man mean about not being able to go back once she discovered her truth? Over time, it again seemed out of her reach.

On the morning of day seven, Constanzia rose early to tend to her goats, all the while going back and forth about whether she should go to the sea. The dreamer in her thought she had nothing to lose and should go. The practical, scared little girl inside her thought it was a waste of time and too dangerous. As she finished her chores, at this point ambivalent about the prospect, Dodger took off running down the same trail that had led them out of the village and down to the sea a week earlier. Constanzia laughed at herself, as she tried to keep up with Dodger. It seemed he was braver than she, and he had decided they were going to the sea. Smiling, she followed his lead.

Out of breath and eager, Constanzia and Dodger arrived at the spot where she had met the old man. Waiting for her was a young woman about her same age, named Elsa. As they introduced themselves to each other, Constanzia's nervousness and fear level started rising.

"How do you know the old man? Is he your grandfather?" Constanzia asked.

Shocked and amazed, Elsa said, "You don't know who Marko is? He is not my grandfather. He is the bravest and wisest person who's ever walked this land. As a matter of fact, he is a legendary warrior who traveled to faraway places to protect this vast land and all its people from invaders."

"Oh, my goodness. I had no idea he was Marko the Brave Warrior! I grew up hearing about him in our folklore. He seemed so frail and old. I would have never guessed that was him. I thought he died a hundred years ago."

Elsa answered, "Yes, he did. But this is a magical place, for those who accept it as so. Marko appears for those who are at a crossroad. Those who are ready will see him."

Constanzia, now more afraid and questioning what she just heard, said, "But I didn't even know I was at a crossroad. And why would he want to come back so old? Are you real?"

Laughing, Elsa replied, "Yes, I am definitely real. Flesh and blood. Marko knew he would not scare you as an old man. Appearing as a warrior would be intimidating. You've been at a crossroad for a while, as you've begun wondering what is beyond the comfort and confines of your village. You are longing for more, and Marko thinks you can benefit from the wisdom shaped by his years of battle and exploration. The wiser he became, the less need he saw to wage physical combat. And yet, he says, one great battle exists."

"I have not heard of any current battles. What battle is that?" Constanzia curiously asked.

"Ah, you have not heard of it, yet the battle lies within you. It is within each of us. It is the struggle between things we want to achieve, and that which keeps us from taking action. But we are getting ahead of ourselves. What would you like to do? Marko sent me here to help you."

Constanzia answered, as if thinking out loud, "I don't know. Part of me gets really excited when I watch the people out there, rowing their boats. And yet part of me is frightened, almost paralyzed at the thought of being out there myself. How bad will my fear get? What if I can't do it? What will the people in my clan say, and how will they react if I am actually able to succeed? I don't know what to do."

"Marko told me you would say that. He sent me here because he saw the potential in you, but it means nothing if I can't help you see it for yourself … to access it. Marko taught me how to discover my truth. If you are willing to trust me, I would be honored to take you through the same process. But first, you need to trust yourself to make the best decision for you. Tell me how much time you need to decide, and I'll meet you back here," Elsa said as she picked up a stone and skipped it across the water, catching Constanzia's attention.

She gasped, as if witnessing more magic, "Oh, no. I am ready now. I don't want to endure this battle any longer. Please, please, help me!"

"Before we get started, you must promise one thing," Elsa said with a serious look and a stern voice. "You must promise that you can do this process without judgment. You can't judge yourself, or others, in any way. This will not be easy. Do you understand me?"

Hesitantly, Constanzia answered, "Um, yes. Yes. I think I know what you mean. Of course, I promise I will not judge anything."

"All right then. The first thing you need to do is build your boat. Follow me." Elsa led Constanzia into the forest to collect wood, vines, resin, and other materials needed to build her boat. Over the next few weeks, as Constanzia followed Elsa's instructions, they would share details about their families, clans, and their upbringing. Constanzia's fear and awkwardness eased with each day.

Finally, her boat was ready. Excited, Constanzia began dragging her boat towards the water's edge, but Elsa yelled, "Not so fast! You must crawl before you can run. Follow me."

They each picked up an end of the boat and carried it over a little hill to a secluded cove of breathtaking beauty. The sand was white and as soft as flour. The water was dark blue-black in color and calm, as if never touched by the wind. The cove was shaped by large hills covered in trees, flowers, and grass, and the color and scent of it all was so vivid it was otherworldly. Constanzia kicked off her shoes, wiggled her toes in the soft sand, opened her arms, and slowly spun to take it all in. "What is this place? Where are we? This is amazing! It's so alive!"

"Come on! Time to learn to crawl!" Elsa shouted as she ran into the calm water.

Constanzia slowly walked in waist deep, as her heart pounded in her chest and adrenaline rushed through her bloodstream. Her first day in the cove was spent breaking through her fear of water and learning how to swim. The next day, Elsa would teach Constanzia how to use the oars she'd carved out of tree limbs. Constanzia quickly mastered swimming, rowing, and maneuvering her boat in the water. It was time for Elsa to leave.

"Constanzia, I will be back here in two days. Spend your time rowing and exploring the waters within the cove. But stay in the cove. Here are some materials, just in case you need to repair your boat. I'll see you soon." With that, Elsa walked towards the far hill, and Constanzia and Dodger headed back to their village.

For the next two days, Constanzia and Dodger would return to the cove. She rowed the waters, while Dodger ate the beautiful flora. Constanzia would pick a landmark across the cove as a target to row to, but invariably ended up with a hole or gash in the boat, forced to row back to shore to make repairs. This went on for two days. Though the first few times it happened she had been very frightened, she was now overcome with frustration. Sitting on the shore, crying softly as she looked out beyond the cove, she realized she had been right all along. She had built a shoddy boat. Venturing out to sea was not meant for people like her. She gave up.

As Elsa walked over the hill, she saw exactly what she'd expected: a frustrated and defeated Constanzia. At this mystical place, it was intended that Constanzia would begin to discover the root of her inner struggle.

"Constanzia, what's wrong?"

Pretending she was okay, she rose to her feet, "I think I built a bad boat. No matter how hard I try, I keep getting holes in it. I'm not cut out for this. It's too hard. I'm going home. Thanks for trying to help me."

Elsa pleaded, "You can't quit now. You've come so far. I know it doesn't feel like it, but you are just about to have a breakthrough. Can you give yourself just one more day? I'm not going to lie to you and say it is always going to be easy, but it is going to be worth it. I promise. Come with me."

They walked together to the water's edge, standing beside the patched-up boat. "Constanzia, you built a fine boat. Your problem is not the boat. It is what's *in* the boat."

"That's impossible! I was the only thing in my boat!" Constanzia said with anger and frustration.

Elsa smiling, "Exactly! If you calm down, I will show you what I mean. Do you want to know?"

Constanzia sighed. "Okay. Go ahead."

"I brought you to The Cove of Enlightenment so that you could become aware of your battle within. If you are ready to discover what's been damaging your boat, and more importantly, impeding your progress, these waters will show you. No one else can do this for you. It's a challenge you will need to take on for yourself. Or … you can turn around now and go back home. You are at a point of no return."

This sounded ominous, and yet a little intriguing. Constanzia took on the challenge. Elsa instructed her to close her eyes, take a few deep breaths, and open her heart and mind, and then when she was ready, to open her eyes and look out over the water.

Constanzia did exactly as instructed. When she opened her eyes again, she held her breath for what came next. Suddenly, an iceberg-shaped mass started to break the surface. And then another, and another. Over the next few minutes, the water filled with these floating masses.

"Wow. What is all that?" she asked in awe.

Elsa, excited that Constanzia had gotten to this point in the process, answered, "This amazing water has the ability to reveal the unseen within you. This is what you've been battling, the cause of your inner struggle. Do you want to go out to see it close up?"

"Can I? Is it safe?" Constanzia wondered aloud.

Elsa nodded. "Yes. Here in this place, you will be safe."

With that, Constanzia pushed her boat into the water and rowed around, observing all the floating masses. Things began to make sense. Each one seemed to represent a fear or a belief she had within her. Some she could recognize, and some were totally foreign. After what seemed like hours, she rowed back to shore.

"Well, what did you discover?" Elsa asked.

"So much. From what I could tell, each one of the masses represents a fear or belief inside of me. Some I was already aware of, and others I was not. Some are good and some are bad."

"Ah, ah, ah. You promised not to judge. Resist the urge to label your fears and beliefs as good or bad," Elsa warned. "You'll know why soon."

"No wonder I couldn't reach any of my targets across the cove. Why do I have so many? And where did they come from?" Constanzia asked.

"We all have a lot. It's just that most people never realize what's keeping them from success. Most of these are from your very early childhood. Remember when we were building your boat, telling each other about our families and clans? We were raised with different beliefs, though some were similar. My people believed the sea was meant to be explored, and yours believed it was a dangerous, treacherous place. We get a lot of our fears from early childhood too, when we are too young to even be aware that it is happening."

Constanzia frowned. "But why would they do that to me, making so many barriers for me to break through?"

Smiling, Elsa said, "They didn't do it *to* you, silly. It's just the way we develop. Some of your fears, which you want to label as bad, were actually meant to keep you safe when you were a child. Remember how they taught us to be afraid of fire, so that we wouldn't play with it and burn ourselves? Then later we had to learn to break through that fear, so that we could build fires for heat and cooking. So, now you need to break through the other fears that are now barriers for you.

"Beliefs are the same way," Elsa continued. "You already have lots of beliefs that help you, like the belief that you are a good person. And like the rest of us, you have beliefs that limit you, that you need to change by questioning them or gaining knowledge."

Standing, Elsa pointed out beyond the opening in the cove to the horizon. "A long, long time ago, my people believed that, if you sailed too close to the horizon, your boat would fall off the world. During that time, no one would dare travel too far from home. Then, after courageous explorers began sailing around the world and returning home, we realized that the world was round. No one in my clan would believe the world is flat today. The belief changed forever."

"Oh! Is that what Marko meant by there is no going back?" Constanzia asked excitedly.

Elsa laughed. "I told you Marko was wise. Yes. Indeed. And that's the good news! You don't have to keep all the stuff those floating masses represent. You can keep what's helping you and build on it by transforming the limiting beliefs into empowering beliefs, and by breaking through the fears that have become barriers."

"How do I do that?" asked Constanzia, now on her feet and eager to get started.

Noticing that Constanzia already looked inspired, Elsa told her, "For the next few weeks, I encourage you to pursue things that you have been too afraid to do in the past. They might be actions, big and small, like climbing a mountain or sharing your feelings in a way that you said is not usual in your family. Be willing to face your fear, no matter the result. Be willing to fall flat on your face, and also to celebrate your results. Pay attention to your emotions, especially ones that limit you. Notice when a limiting belief appears and question it, challenge it, and create a new empowering belief. It sounds like a lot, but it will become second nature for you once you start tapping into the courage within yourself. Let's meet back here in a month."

What a day! Constanzia and Dodger headed back to the village but first stopped at the shore of the sea where she had met Marko. She watched the explorers, as they headed out to sea, feeling filled with possibility for her own future. She felt like anything was possible.

For the next few weeks, Constanzia did as instructed, taking on every opportunity that came her way and searching for new things to conquer. She talked her older brother into taking her on his trip to climb the highest mountain peak on the land. He thought for sure she would chicken out, but she mustered the courage to finish, even when she was terrified to continue.

She asked for help in learning to do new things around the village, which she never would have had the courage to do before. She traveled out of her village to meet new people and open herself up to them. After a few weeks, some of her family noticed a change in her, saying she seemed more confident. Constanzia set her sights on one last challenge before returning to the cove.

She'd always had a fear of speaking in front of a lot of people, a fear of being seen. But she was so happy that she didn't want to keep her secret any longer. She wanted to gather her entire clan together and tell them about meeting Marko and the changes she was making in her life. The thought of this left her paralyzed. Every time she thought she was ready to gather everyone, she was overcome with fear.

Over a few days of thinking about it, and feeling fear on and off, she came to realize that she also had a belief that nobody wanted to hear what she had to say. Could her belief and her fear be connected? Constanzia began to challenge that belief. As far as she knew, no one else in her clan had met Marko. But she had. She had been to the sea and come to know it as an exciting place of adventure and beauty, very different from the way her people described it. She realized that she knew a lot of things that, just maybe, they didn't know. Perhaps she would be able to expand their world by sharing what she had experienced. *Yes,* she thought. *They DO need to hear what I have to say.*

This would be her biggest challenge yet … and another point from which there would be no turning back.

It was the evening before Constanzia was set to return to the cove to meet Elsa, and she had called everyone in her clan together. Now they were seated on the ground in a large field on the edge of the village. Standing on a tree stump, she nervously looked out over the familiar faces, all waiting for her to speak. Her voice was shaky as she began to share her story about meeting Marko. To her surprise, instead of getting up and leaving, they stayed on the grass, giving her their full attention. The more she shared, the more they wanted to know.

As it turned out, they had heard of Marko sightings, but they had thought it didn't happen to people like them. They thought it happened only to more elevated clans. They were in awe that Marko had found one of their people worthy of this experience. She had showed them all that it was possible for them too. They just needed to believe it and be willing to move outside of the comfort zone of their village … and face their fear.

That night, she had the best sleep ever, and the next day, she returned to The Cove of Enlightenment. When she arrived, Elsa was waiting for her, anxious to hear every detail of what she had learned. Constanzia told her about all the fears she'd faced, the new things she'd tried, all the things she'd learned about herself, and how her experience had changed her people.

Thrilled with this news, Elsa asked, "Are you ready to revisit the battle within yourself? Surely you are interested in seeing the results. I know you can already feel them."

"Yes! Let's do it!" Constanzia shouted as she closed her eyes, took a few deep breaths, and opened her heart and mind. When she was ready, she opened her eyes and looked out over the water of the cove.

Over the next few minutes, masses began breaking the surface, but they were no longer huge like icebergs. There were fewer of the masses, and the ones that did appear were more like ice floes, floating along the surface.

The water, which had once been a darkly opaque blue-black color, was now crystal-clear turquoise. They could see all the way to the bottom of the cove. Constanzia jumped into her boat to get an up-close look. She noticed how easily she could navigate to the other side of the cove now, where it had been impossible for her to reach previously. The masses remaining in the cove were much more manageable for her.

As she rowed back, she saw Elsa and Dodger standing at the shore, waiting for her. Pulling her boat onto the sand, with tears in her eyes, she thanked Elsa for helping her discover her truth: that she had everything within her to break through her own barriers to success. She now understood how much all that stuff had been holding her back, and how clearly she could maneuver through life with this deeper understanding of herself. She now knew her truth, and there was no turning back to her old self.

Sensing someone behind her, she turned to see Marko, the old man, beaming with pride as he looked out over the cove and then back to Constanzia, with Dodger chewing the back of his sweater once more.

"It looks like you did a great job, Constanzia. How do you feel?"

"I feel invincible!" she exclaimed.

Marko nodded, smiling. "Indeed, you are. Looks like my work here is done. Enjoy your newfound, inspired courage!" Marko turned then and slowly started to walk away. After a few steps, he stopped, turned back, and said, "By the way ... you owe me a sweater."

With a wink and a smile, he vanished.

Acknowledgments

A lthough I kept the writing of this book under wraps until my manuscript was complete, it would be disingenuous to take sole credit for this project. The others who helped make this book possible (most of them unknowingly) have come into my life with divine timing and order. Each has been instrumental in shaping and preparing me to do the work that I do, ultimately leading to the creation of this book. I am compelled to shout from the rooftop to give each the credit they deserve.

My parents, Tim and Kaye Phelan, showed me how to play by the rules and value hard work and honesty. (Yes, a white lie is still a lie!) My dad's love of sports was contagious and helped instill discipline, a drive to be the best, and the value of teamwork. I'm grateful for the opportunities you provided me. Thank you for giving me the space and freedom to grow and unconditional love for the woman I grew into.

To the most positive human being I have ever met, Karen E. Pfeffer. I would not be who I am today without you opening my eyes to a more positive way of being. You have been the igniter of so many challenges I have taken on, and to so much I have accomplished. This book is no exception, as you encouraged me and patiently listened as I read each chapter aloud. You have also been a partner in so many of the stories within this book. As my biggest cheerleader, you *always* believed in me until I finally believed the impossible was possible, time and again. This has been an incredible journey we have been on for the past twenty-three years, and I can't wait to see what's next. My love, thank you for being my better half, and for making me a better human. I so appreciate your unconditional love and unwavering support.

"Friend" does not seem an adequate title for John Schroeder, who (along with Karen) has been with me on this journey since day one. Firewalk participants will know John as the man behind the camera and the guy tending to the fire. But I know John from my days in printing, and as a person who has grown with me by being a willing accomplice on so many insane adventures. He has been an integral part of the thousands of breakthroughs I have facilitated. John, you are a friend in the truest sense, and I am eternally grateful for your friendship, love, and support. Looking forward to our next adventure!

Amantha Murphy, who carries the stories and wisdom of Ireland, helped me have a deeper understanding of myself. Through years of personal work and travel in Ireland, she helped me find my life's purpose and discover my hidden gifts and talents. By her example, I learned to hold space for people as they work through their process of change. Thank you, Amantha. Many, many people have been helped through the wisdom you have imparted to me. *"Go raibh maith agat a chara!"* (And thank you as well to Patricia J. Quinn, who led me to Amantha.)

My eternal gratitude to Dr. Karen E. Peterson, the most skilled and compassionate psychologist a lost soul could ever hope for. I am here today because of you and my family is forever changed.

I offer sincere gratitude to Lou Agudo, Stephanie McKinley, Shannon Hoots Cid, and Frank Cid for allowing me the honor of working with your clients in addiction recovery. They kept me on my toes, and I grew immensely from my work with them. They taught me as much as I taught them—especially about the human condition and what it means to truly overcome. I am a better person because of each of you, as well as every person in addiction recovery I have encountered.

Lisa LaJoie was the impetus for the writing of this book during the coronavirus pandemic. First telling me I should write it, then insisting that I do. Like the wise woman she is, she negated my laughing and all the reasons why "I can't" by asking, "What the hell else do you have to do?" Thank you, Lisa, for the insightful question that cut through the B.S. of my belief system, and for introducing me to Les, the man who would help me make it happen.

I have been blessed with great coaches and teachers, and Les Kletke fits the mold. He coached me through my writing process with the patience of a saint, the wisdom of a sage, and humor and wit to match my own. Les brought out the best in me, even when I was at my worst. He stayed steady, encouraging, and believed in my ability to write a book I could be proud of long before I believed it myself. I looked forward to our weekly calls, when Les would, through effortless conversation, bring my next topic to the surface and dig for the story, as well as for important points for the reader. He understood the work that I do and my audience, which I also found valuable during the publishing process. Les, my friend, thank you for coaching this book to life.

An adventure in Northern Ireland that culminated with a walk across the Carrick-a-Rede rope bridge made Sharie Falk and I fast friends. Little did I know at the time that, a year and a half later, she would be fact-checking psychological theory on a book that I didn't know I would write. Just goes to show the serendipity of life. Thank you for sharing your expertise and knowledge with me.

To the team at FriesenPress, thank you for your guidance. With a special thank you to Cam Bradley and Tiffany Zemlak for keeping me on track and to my editors Janet Layberry and Jessica Torrens, wonderful wordsmiths.

Thank you to all the clients I have had the opportunity to work with, and for trusting me with your teams. I am especially grateful to those of you who took a chance on an unknown early on in my career.

And finally, I want to extend a heartfelt thank you to all the people I have had the honor to work with in facilitating your breakthroughs. I am humbled by your trust in me. I remain in awe when I see the remarkable things people accomplish when they have the courage to embrace their fears!

Get your team fired up!

To learn how Connie Phelan and Fire Power Seminars can
propel you and your organization to new levels of success,
write to connie@firepowerseminars.com or
visit www.firepowerseminars.com
Experience the breakthrough.

About the Author

Connie Phelan has been a teenage athlete, dedicated employee and an entrepreneur, beginning her professional career working in the world of printing and advertising, but in all these roles her greatest barriers and limitations came from within. Fear and self-limiting beliefs, which she had carried with her since childhood, had always held her back—even when she didn't realize they were doing so. It wasn't until she was (reluctantly) exposed to a new way of being during a personal-development seminar that she broke through her own fears and her life began to change.

In 2006, inspired by her own transformative experience, she became the founder and CEO of Fire Power Seminars, and as a speaker and facilitator has worked with thousands of individuals from all walks of life, ranging from leaders and employees within organizations and companies both large and small—including Fortune 500s, universities, athletes, and people in addiction recovery. A certified firewalk instructor, as well as a certified neuro-linguistic programming practitioner, she has a passion for helping people discover potential they never knew they had, so they can start living their best lives.

Starting from a place of caution and self-doubt in Fort Lauderdale—Connie now lives in Atlanta with her partner and four-legged family members, and enjoys "adventure travel," snow-covered mountains, and chasing the northern lights.

www.firepowerseminars.com

CPSIA information can be obtained
at www.ICGtesting.com
Printed in the USA
BVHW081452190722
642490BV00012B/658